THE FOUNTAINWELL DRAMA TEXTS

General Editors

ARTHUR BROWN

T. A. DUNN

JOHN HORDEN

A. NORMAN JEFFARES

BRIAN W. M. SCOBIE

3

GEORGE FARQUHAR

THE
BEAUX STRATAGEM

Edited by
A. NORMAN JEFFARES

OLIVER & BOYD
EDINBURGH
1972

OLIVER AND BOYD
Tweeddale Court
14 High Street
Edinburgh EH1 1YL
(A Division of Longman Group Ltd)

First Published 1972

Hardback   05   001573   7
Paperback   05   001691   1

Printed in Great Britain by
T. & A. CONSTABLE LTD, Hopetoun Street
Edinburgh

ACKNOWLEDGMENTS

For assistance and advice in the preparation of this edition I am greatly indebted to my colleague Mr John Horden, and to the former Assistant General Editor of the Fountainwell Drama Texts, now my colleague at Leeds, Mr Brian W. M. Scobie. Mr D. G. Neill of the Bodleian Library and Mr R. J. Roberts of the British Museum have been most helpful to me in bibliographical matters. Miss Mary Ann Jensen, Curator of the Theatre Collection, Princeton University Library, Mr Arnold Wengrow, Theatre Collection, Harvard University Library, and Mr David Masson, Brotherton Collection, University of Leeds Library, have all given generous aid.

Leeds   A. N. J.
December 1971

CONTENTS

CRITICAL INTRODUCTION   1

A NOTE ON THE TEXT   17

THE BEAUX STRATAGEM   21

TEXTUAL NOTES   109

COMMENTARY   115

BIBLIOGRAPHY   123

CRITICAL INTRODUCTION

The Beaux Stratagem is Farquhar's last and best play. He wrote it at the instigation of his friend Robert Wilks the actor, who called on him at his lodgings in York Buildings about the middle of December 1706 only to find Farquhar had moved to a cheaper garret in St Martin's Lane. At the time the young Irish playwright was in debt, miserable— "heart-broken" in his own words—and extremely ill. Wilks gave him twenty guineas, urged him to write another play, and promised to call in a week to see its framework. Within six weeks Farquhar had finished the comedy, though he rewrote parts of it up to its production. It is likely that his illness was tuberculosis; before he had finished the second act he is said to have "felt death upon him": he managed, however, to resume work and *The Beaux Stratagem*, with all its lively gaiety, is a monument to his courage and determination as well as to his sense of humour and his ability to innovate. He died in his thirtieth year, in May 1707, and was buried on 23 May.[1]

The sources for the play are several and are both literary and autobiographical. Cervantes probably provided the basic idea of an inn in *Don Quixote*, but *via* Jean de la Chapelle's *Les Carosses d'Orleans*, which Farquhar, in collaboration with Peter Motteaux, had adapted as *The Stage Coach* (1704). Some of the ideas in *The Stage Coach* are developed in *The Beaux Stratagem*. Farquhar's recruiting tour of 1705, during which he visited Lichfield and Shrewsbury, provided him with other material for the scenes of the play and its characters. Just as he had written *The Recruiting Officer* (1706) out of his experience of Shrewsbury, now he turned to his memories of Lichfield. He had stayed at the George Inn there, and its landlord, John Harrison, gave him ideas for Bonniface the innkeeper. Harrison's daughter perhaps served as a model for Cherry, Bonniface's daughter, though she may also be founded upon Dolly in *The Stage Coach*.[2]

[1] See Eric Rothstein, *George Farquhar*, pp. 28–9. New York (Twayne) 1967.
[2] See Thomas Harwood, *The History and Antiquities of the Church and City of Lichfield*, p. 501. Gloucester 1806.

Farquhar became friendly with Sir Michael Biddulph on his recruiting tour and frequently visited him and his family at Elmhurst. This was a large and charming country house outside Lichfield, which was probably a model for Lady Bountiful's house, just as Sir Michael's humorous servant, Thomas Bond, inspired the creation of Scrub, Sullen's servant. Farquhar enjoyed the company of Sir Michael's family: two of his children, the daughters of his first marriage, were just out of their teens; and there were three others by his second wife, who may herself have provided material for the character of Lady Bountiful. Lichfield also contained French officers who were prisoners of war and presumably lent themselves to the portrait of Count Bellair. Foigard, the Irish character, a type Farquhar had drawn before in Macahone in *The Stage Coach*, and earlier in Teague in *The Twin-Rivals* (1703), was founded upon an actual Father Fogarty or "Fogourdy" mentioned by Pepys in February 1664.

The play owed something to Vanbrugh's work. The concept of an ill-assorted husband and wife in *The Provok'd Wife* is developed in *The Beaux Stratagem*. Sir John Brute, who comes home roaring drunk and disturbs his wife when she is asleep,[3] seems a mild rehearsal for Farquhar's Squire Sullen who returns at four in the morning to "flounce into Bed, dead as a Salmon into a Fishmonger's Basket; his Feet cold as Ice, his Breath hot as a Furnace, and his Hands and his Face as greasy as his Flanel Night-cap" [11. 1. 65-7]. Vanbrugh also depicts the situation of an ill-assorted pair in *The Relapse*, where Berinthia makes a speech[4], in which she describes the differences between her late husband's interests and her own. She is, however, a different kind of woman from Farquhar's Mrs Sullen. In *The Relapse* when Loveless enters Berinthia's chamber her protests are mild and he ravishes her off stage. But, when this situation of the lover concealed in the lady's bedroom is repeated in *The Beaux Stratagem*, Mrs Sullen, though greatly taken with Archer, shrieks violently, and the seduction does not occur.

This is symptomatic of the change which occurs between the drama of Vanbrugh and Farquhar. Farquhar reflects a shift in sensibility. He has an Elizabethan vitality: but though he moves away from the Restoration comedy of manners he is not moving completely into sentimental comedy. Just as he places his plays in the country, just as

---

[3] Vanbrugh, *The Provok'd Wife*, III. III.
[4] Vanbrugh, *The Relapse*, II. I.

he turns from the wit and repartee of Restoration court drama towards an easier eighteenth-century dialogue, so he tackles, head on, a moral situation new in the drama: the question of divorce. His own un-satisfactory marriage, which took place in 1703, may well have prompted his reading of Milton's *Doctrine and Discipline of Divorce* when he wrote *The Beaux Stratagem*. Margaret Parnell, a thirty-five year old widow with two children, had deceived him by pretending she had an income of £500 a year. Farquhar had been in debt when he married her, but even the good fortune of the Lieutenant's commission which he gained in 1704 was not enough to keep him and his new family, to which he had speedily added two daughters. His illness depressed him and despite the success of *The Recruiting Officer* in 1706, he was deeply worried about the future of his children, for he was still in debt, possibly as a result of spending his own money on the recruit-ing expedition. It is possible that his own marital situation lent greater intensity to his dramatic investigation of a situation where an ill-assorted husband and wife dislike each other and wish to separate. As in his other plays, he put a good deal of himself into the main character, Aimwell, though Archer, the other young man in search of money through marriage, is also reminiscent of some aspects of Farquhar's own personality. (There is only one passage of bitterness in the play—that in which they discuss Jack Generous who is avoided "for no Crime upon Earth but the want of Money" [I. I. 147-8].) But though his own energy and his regard for the ladies inform the young men, he is also deeply influenced by Milton. Archer, for instance, describes his flirtation with Cherry in Miltonic tones:

> The Nymph that with her twice ten hundred Pounds
> With brazen Engine hot, and Quoif clear starch'd
> Can fire the Guest in warming of the Bed . . .

There's a Touch of Sublime *Milton* for you, and the Subject but an Inn-keeper's Daughter. [III. II. 22-6].

Milton was a direct influence on the situation between Sullen and his wife. This passage between them is one of economical hatred:

SULLEN. You're impertinent.
MRS SULLEN. I was ever so, since I became one Flesh with you.

SULLEN. One Flesh! rather two Carcasses join'd unnaturally together.

MRS SULLEN. Or rather a living Soul coupled to a dead Body. [III. III. 276-281].

It derives from the second book of Milton's *Doctrine and Discipline of Divorce*:

> nay, instead of being one flesh, they will be rather two carcasses chained unnaturally together; or, as it may happen, a living soul bound to a dead corpse.[5]

And when Dorinda tells Mrs Sullen that the divisions between her husband and herself don't come within reach of the law for a divorce Mrs Sullen bursts into heartfelt speech:

> Law! what Law can search into the remote Abyss of Nature, what Evidence can prove the unaccountable Disaffections of Wedlock—can a Jury sum up the endless Aversions that are rooted in our Souls, or can a Bench give Judgment upon Antipathies. [III. III. 414-8].

She appeals to Nature, the first lawgiver, who when she has "set Tempers opposite not all the golden Links of Wedlock, nor Iron Manacles of law can keep 'um fast". This dialogue, with its appeal to Nature, echoes Milton's general account of the evils of natural hatred and has taken over his phrases, as, for instance, in this sentence:

> To couple hatred therefore, though wedlock try all her golden links, and borrow to her aid all the iron manacles and fetters of the law, it does but seek to twist a rope of sand.[6]

Again, when Sullen accidentally meets his wife's brother, Sir Charles Freeman, for the first time in the Inn, their discussion contains further echoes of Milton on the subject. Milton's views that the greatest

---

[5] Milton, *Doctrine and Discipline of Divorce*, in *Prose Works*, ed. J. A. St. John, (1848–74) III, p. 249. See Martin A. Larson, "The Influence of Milton's Divorce Tracts on Farquhar's *Beaux' Stratagem*," in *P.M.L.A.*, XXXIX (1924), pp. 174–8.

[6] Milton, *op. cit.*, III, p. 265.

breach of marriage is unfitness of mind, that there is no true marriage between those who agree not in true consent of mind and that the unity of mind is nearer and greater than the union of bodies—are formulated in compressed form by Sir Charles in answer to a query of Bonniface's when the Innkeeper asks "Are not Man and Wife one Flesh?":

> SIR CHARLES. You and your Wife, Mr. Guts, may be one Flesh, because ye are nothing else—but rational Creatures have minds that must be united.
> SULLEN. Minds.
> SIR CHARLES. Ay, minds, Sir, don't you think that the Mind takes place of the Body? [v. i. 58-63].

This attitude to divorce as a subject for drama was new, and so was Farquhar's picture of the unhappy yet loyal wife. Mrs Sullen's view of Archer is honest:

> I do love that Fellow;—And if I met him drest as he shou'd be, and I undrest as I shou'd be—Look'ye, Sister, I have no supernatural Gifts;—I can't swear I cou'd resist the Temptation,—tho' I can safely promise to avoid it; and that's as much as the best of us can do. [IV. I. 447-451].

And yet she does resist. This marks a departure from the libertinism of the Restoration court dramatists, but it is a realistic one. The characters are not what they seem; neither she nor her husband see each other as they are; and some of the other characters surprise us too: even Scrub, for instance, has an abundant simplicity with which to conceal his cunning.

The names of the characters indicate something of their nature. The name of Count Bellair suggests how different his manner will be from that of Sullen, a name which so suits the squire. His wife's maiden name was Freeman, and freedom from the sullen temper of her husband is what she seeks. Lady Bountiful has given her name to the phrase "to play Lady Bountiful": it was well conceived as a name for a countrywoman who is "one of the best of Women", laying out half her income "in charitable Uses for the Good of her Neighbours", and curing people of illness.

Cherry's name suggests her bright manner, and Gipsey's her wild one, while Dorinda is a suitable name (this is an early use of it) for the young woman who is a stock heroine. Aimwell, her lover, is well named for the effect Farquhar wanted to create, of a wild young man who none the less intends well, is generous, and honest. Archer, his friend, is more of a Restoration rogue-hero: his name is stressed twice in the play: in II. II. 40 he remarks "Let me alone, for I am a Mark'sman" and in III. II. 1, Archer takes up the point "Well, *Tom*, I find you're a Marksman". The imagery is that of military aggression and amorous attack. No scruples restrain his pursuit of maid or matron; he is more apt to deceive; he is quiverful of amorous energy:

> I can be charm'd with *Sappho's* singing without falling in Love with her Face; I love Hunting, but wou'd not, like *Acteon*, be eaten up by my own Dogs; I love a fine House, but let another keep it; and just so I love a fine Woman. [I. I. 219-222].

The stock villains are likewise indicated by their names. Gibbet is clear enough: the names of Hounslow and Bagshot are perhaps suggested by the heaths which were infested by highwaymen. Bonniface's name suits his trade as innkeeper: his duplicity is part of the deceiving which goes on; the name soon appears ironic and contributes to the stratagem of the play, where appearances are specious.

Surprise is one of the elements that Farquhar built into *The Beaux Stratagem*: its construction is skilful. He is again contrasting city and country, contrasting life in the inn and in the house, the honest lover and the less scrupulous, the sottish Sullen and the polished Count Bellair, the innocent Dorinda and realistic Mrs Sullen. The plot revolves around deception. In the first act we learn about the designs of Aimwell and Archer, a fortune-hunting and flirting pair of impoverished young men. The next act tells us clearly that Mrs Sullen's marriage is intolerable: she is flirting with Count Bellair—to revenge herself upon her husband; this is her stratagem, but one set within wishful limits. We learn that Bonniface and his highwaymen friends are deceivers also and plan to rob Lady Bountiful. The third Act gives us the lovers' views of each other; Mrs Sullen and Dorinda have observed Archer and Aimwell in church with some interest, and Aimwell has fallen in love with Dorinda. The plot becomes more complex and the action livens up with the introduction of Foigard. Scrub fears Foigard's relations with Gipsey the maid; Mrs Sullen has begun to think of Archer rather than Count Bellair; and Dorinda becomes interested in Aimwell. The tempo of the action accelerates sharply as Count Bellair's wooing of Mrs Sullen is interrupted: she draws a pistol on him—and on Sullen who bursts in on them and ruthlessly expresses his indifference as to how she behaves provided she does not misbehave with a Frenchman. The third act moves from a gay picture of love and intrigue to an examination of the intolerable nature of unhappy marriage.

The fourth act speeds up the action even more with Aimwell, who is pretending to be his brother Lord Aimwell, feigning illness in Lady Bountiful's house, and thus managing to propose to Dorinda while Archer makes propositions to Mrs Sullen. The plot is complicated further by Foigard's bribing Gipsey to hide Count Bellair in Mrs Sullen's closet. Archer replaces him, having blackmailed Foigard by threatening to reveal him as an Irishman serving with the French army. The highwaymen arrive to rob the house at midnight.

The final act resolves the situation, though not as simply as might have been expected. Mrs Sullen's brother, Sir Charles Freeman, meets Sullen at the Inn; their frank discussion prepares us for the subsequent solution of the situation between the Sullens. Aimwell is told by Cherry of the plot and he arrives to fight two of the thieves while Archer, foiled in his attempt on Mrs Sullen by the entry of Scrub when she shrieked, has overcome another of them in Mrs Sullen's room. He aids Aimwell and urges him—once the highwaymen are consigned to the cellar—to marry Dorinda at once, with Foigard at hand to conduct the service. Archer himself attempts to trade on his wound in order to resume his advances to Mrs Sullen. But then all this stratagem seems likely to fail, for Sir Charles Freeman, who knows Archer in London, is announced.

The complications continue. Aimwell tells Dorinda he is not Lord Aimwell. But Dorinda hears from Sir Charles that Aimwell's brother is dead; he *is* Lord Aimwell. Archer now demands half Dorinda's fortune in view of his earlier arrangement with Aimwell; but Aimwell offers him it all because of his own new wealth. Sir Charles enters; he intends to arrange for his sister to part from Sullen and all agree to aid him. Then Sullen comes on the scene; and he and Mrs Sullen, after their doxology of hatred, agree to part. Sullen, however, will not give up her dowry, whereupon Count Bellair offers to pay a dowry and take Mrs Sullen away. But the total sum involved (£10,000) appals him. Then Archer offers to pay it. He can resolve the situation since he has taken from one of the highwaymen all the contents of Sullen's escritoire, "all the Writings of your Estate, all the Articles of Marriage with his Lady, Bills, Bonds, Leases, Receipts to an infinite Value". Cherry becomes maid to Dorinda, and Archer and Mrs Sullen round off the play by leading a dance. The play echoes Milton to the end, extolling divorce by mutual consent in the name of freedom:

> Both happy in their several States we find,
> Those parted by consent, and those conjoin'd,
> Consent, if mutual, saves the Lawyer's Fee,
> Consent is Law enough to set you free, [v. IV. 288-291].

II. CRITICAL RECEPTION

The Muses Mercury, in May 1707, contained an early assessment of Farquhar's merits as a dramatist, whose last two plays "had something in them that was truly humorous and diverting". The comment, probably by John Oldmixon, continues in a patronising way:

> 'Tis true the Critiks will not allow any Part of them to be regular; but *Mr Farquhar* had a Genius for Comedy, of which one may say that it was rather above Rules than below them. His Conduct, tho not artful, was *surpriȝing*; his *characters*, tho not Great, were just, his Humour, tho *low*, diverting; His *Dialogue*, tho *loose* and *incorrect*, *gay* and *agreeable*; and His Wit, tho not *super-abundant*, *pleasant*. In a word, his Plays have in the *toute ensemble*, as the Painters phrase it, a certain *Novelty* and *Mirth*, which pleas'd the Audience every time they were represented; And such as love to laugh at the *Theater*, will probably miss him more than they now imagine.[7]

The comment on his "low" humour was echoed by Pope's description of his "pert low dialogue". But, though his dialogue may have seemed low to middle-class audiences in the eighteenth century, it had a buoyancy about it which Goldsmith (some of whose own work was

[7] Text from Charles Stonehill's edition of *The Complete Works of George Farquhar* (1930), I, XXXI. (The British Museum copy of *The Muses Mercury* was destroyed by bombing.)

also regarded as "low") greatly appreciated. Kate Hardcastle, for instance, in *She Stoops to Conquer*, is made to ask "Don't you think I look something like Cherry in *The Beaux Stratagem?*"[8] And the plot of *She Stoops to Conquer* owes a good deal to *The Beaux Stratagem*. Farquhar, however, had realised that it was necessary to learn from an enemy; his Preface to *The Twin-Rivals* (1703) made clear his desire to avoid the condemnation for low morals that his predecessors had earned: "*The Success and Countenance that Debauchery has met with in Plays was the most Severe and Reasonable Charge against their Authors in Mr* Collier's short View." Farquhar was a link between the older Restoration writers and Steele, Cibber, Kelly, Cumberland, Goldsmith and Sheridan; but Mrs Inchbald was warning the reader in her "Remarks" (which accompanied an edition of 1808) that though he might be charmed with the spirit of Archer and Aimwell:

> those two fine gentlemen are but arrant impostors; and that the lively, though pitiable Mrs Sullen, is no other than a deliberate violator of her marriage vow. Highly delighted with every character he will not, perhaps, at first observe, that all the wise and witty persons of this comedy are knaves, and all the honest people fools.[9]

She thought the well-drawn characters, happy incidents and excellent dialogue "but poor atonement from that unrestrained contempt of principle which pervades every scene". Leigh Hunt wrote in 1818 that Farquhar's love of sympathy "which he degraded in his dramas into mere dissipation, might have opened his eyes to discover 'the soul of goodness' in things which he found evil, and which he left so".[10] And the following year Hazlitt remarked that the decline of English comedy might be dated "from the time of Farquhar". Hazlitt, however, had good-will towards Farquhar's heroes, and wrote that:

> We seem to like both the author and his favourites. He has humour, character, and invention in common with the other, with a more unaffected gaiety and spirit of enjoyment, which overflows

---

[8] *She Stoops to Conquer*, III. I.

[9] Mrs Inchbald, "Remarks", in *The British Theatre*, vol. 8, 1808.

[10] *Leigh Hunt's Dramatic Criticism*, ed. L. H. Houtchens and C. W. Houtchens, New York (Columbia University Press) 1949. p. 207.

and sparkles in all he does. He makes us laugh from pleasure
oftener than from malice. He somewhere prides himself in having
introduced on the stage the class of comic heroes here spoken of,
which has since become a standard character, and which re-
presents the warm hearted rattle-brained thoughtless, high-
spirited young fellow, who floats on the back of his misfortunes
without repining, who forfeits appearances, but saves his honour;
and he gives us to understand that it was his own. He did not
need to be ashamed of it. Indeed there is internal evidence that
this sort of character is his own, for it pervades his works
generally, and is the moving spirit that informs them. His
comedies have on this account probably a greater appearance of
truth and nature than almost any others. His incidents succeed
one another with rapidity, but without premeditation; his wit is
easy and spontaneous; his style animated, unembarrassed, and
flowing; his characters full of life and spirit, and never unrestrained so as to "overstep the modesty of nature", though they
sometimes, from haste and carelessness, seem left in a crude un-
finished state. There is a constant ebullition of gay, laughing
invention, cordial good humour, and fine animal spirits, in his
writings.[11]

This was well said, and timely. Lamb's essay "On the artificial
comedy of the last century" was less directly concerned with Farquhar
and took the line of regarding the conventions of Restoration Drama as
sui generis.

In *A History of Eighteenth Century Literature* (*1660–1780*) (1889)
Edmund Gosse was appreciative of Farquhar as "the last great dramatist of the Restoration" and in 1892 he described him—somewhat on
Hazlitt's lines—as "of a loving disposition, and as inflammable as a
hayrick".[12] Louise Imogen Guiney was sympathetic, if not profound,
in *A Little English Gallery* (1894) but this reasonable account of
Farquhar's work was followed by A. W. Ward's priggish caution in *A
History of English Dramatic Literature* (1899), where some of the
incidents of *The Beaux Stratagem* were "of dubious import, including
one at the close—a separation by mutual consent—which throws a

[11] Hazlitt, *Lectures on the English Comic Writers*. London 1819. Text quoted
here from *Works* (1894), p. 112.
[12] Gosse, *Gossip in a Library*, London 1892. p. 155.

glaring light on the view taken by the author and his age of the sanctity of the marriage tie".

The first serious study of Farquhar's life, D. Schmid's *George Farquhar, Sein Leben und Seine Original Dramen*, was published in Vienna in 1904. In this biography Dr Schmid first pointed out that Farquhar had set the action of his plays in the provinces. Earlier biographical material had been included in the Sixth Edition of the *Works* (1728) as "some memories of Mr George Farquhar" told by Robert Wilks to W. R. Chetwood, and a *Life* by T. Wilkes was included in the three-volume Dublin edition of the *Works* (1775). This contained an account of Farquhar's death, apparently obtained from Colley Cibber but actually from W. R. Chetwood, *A General History of the Stage* (1749). Other biographical information appeared in William Egerton's *Faithful Memoirs of . . . Mrs Anne Oldfield* (1731), in Daniel O'Bryan's *Authentic Memoir; or, the Life, and Character of that most celebrated Comedian Mr Robert Wilks* (1732) and in Edmund Curll's *The Life of that Eminent Comedian Robert Wilks, Esq.* (1733).

Charles Whibley wrote an article in the *Cambridge History of English Literature* (1912), pp. 169–73 which is still useful, but J. E. Palmer's *The Comedy of Manners* (1913) now seems dated, even gloomy in its view that Farquhar was born too late and never bridged the gulf between personal convictions and moral and artistic conventions. He thought that Farquhar "killed the comedy to which he contributed the last brilliant examples" (p. 242).

There were accounts of Farquhar's work in George Henry Nettleton's *English Drama of the Restoration and Eighteenth Century (1642–1780)* (1914) and E. Bernbaum, *The Drama of Sensibility* (1915), while William Archer's *The Old Drama and the New* (1923) regarded Farquhar's work as possessing "a general tone of humanity which is far above the level of the preceding age". He attacked Sir Adolphus Ward who had written of Farquhar's coarseness of fibre, and pointed out that his morality was distinctly above the general Restoration level and grew progressively better through his brief career; he thought a sane criticism of life began to appear in Farquhar and Steele and he attacked Ward's view of the final incident of Mrs Sullen's separation:

> We have in this comedy a serious and very damaging criticism of the conventional view that there can be no immorality in marriage save breach of the marriage vow. The scenes between

Mrs Sullen and Dorinda at the end of Act III and between Squire
Sullen and Sir Charles Freeman at the beginning of Act V, are
a plea for what Farquhar regarded, rightly or wrongly, as a more
rational law of divorce.[13]

He distinguished between Farquhar and the earlier comic dramatists,
Wycherley, Congreve and Vanbrugh: they were both social essay-
ists and dramatists with their roles imperfectly differentiated, but
Farquhar was a dramatist and nothing else, and he widened the range of
comedy.

Bonamy Dobrée's *Restoration Comedy* (1924) continued the process
of sensible evaluation of Farquhar's plays and conveyed some of its
author's enjoyment of Farquhar's sense of fun. Allardyce Nicoll's *A
History of English Drama* (1924; revd. 1952) paid due tribute to
Farquhar as a "link between Congreve and Cibber" while Joseph
Wood Krutch in *Comedy and Conscience after the Restoration* (1924)
saw Farquhar as a consistent adherent to the old belief that realism and
satire rather than sentiment and morality were the business of comedy.
H. Ten Eyck Perry in *The Comic Spirit in Restoration Drama* (1925),
regarded Archer as "the last effort of the Comedy of Manners to
maintain its position in the teeth of Jeremy Collier and Eighteenth
Century propriety".

K. M. Lynch, *The Social Mode of Restoration Comedy* (1926) and
J. H. Smith, *The Gay Couple in Restoration Comedy* (1948), and T. H.
Fujimara, *The Restoration Comedy of Wit* (1952) all deal sensibly with
Farquhar.

Farquhar's life was written with skill and sympathy by Willard
Connely in *Young George Farquhar, The Restoration Drama at
Twilight* (1949), a book which has become the standard biography.
There is a very good brief life in Frederick S. Boas, *An Introduction to
Eighteenth Century Drama 1700–1780* (1953). Contemporary critic-
ism has been enhanced by A. J. Farmer's concise *George Farquhar*
(1966) in the *Writers and their Work* series, and by Eric Rothstein's
excellent *George Farquhar* (1967).

Various editions of Farquhar's works have been published. Leigh
Hunt's edition of *The Dramatic Works of Wycherley, Congreve,
Vanbrugh and Farquhar* (1840) was followed by A. C. Ewald's two-

[13] W. Archer, *The Old Drama and the New*, pp. 209–210. London (Heinemann)
1923.

volume edition of *The Dramatic Works of George Farquhar* (1892). These editions were emended by William Archer in *George Farquhar* (1906), a collection containing *The Constant Couple*, *The Twin–Rivals*, The *Recruiting Officer*, and *The Beaux Stratagem*. A little-known but excellent and trenchantly edited text of *The Beaux Stratagem* is that by H. M. Fitzgibbon (1898). *The Complete Works of George Farquhar*, two vols. (1930) edited by Charles Stonehill is full of useful information, with texts based on the first edition, with new material on the life, and with other material not previously printed. *British Dramatists from Dryden to Sheridan*, ed. G. H. Nettleton and A. E. Case (1939) contains a well-edited version of *The Beaux Stratagem*.

The *Beaux Stratagem* has been translated as *Die Stuzerlist* by J. Leonhardi (Berlin, 1782); as *Le Stratagème des Roués* by M. Constantin-Weyer (Paris, 1921); as *La Strattagemma dei Bellimbusti* by A. Lombardo (Florence, 1955); and as *La Ruse des Galants* by J. Hamard (Paris, 1965).

III. STAGE HISTORY

1. *In the British Isles*

The *Beaux Stratagem* was first performed at the Queen's Theatre, Haymarket on 8 Mar. 1707 with Wilks as Archer and Anne Oldfield as Mrs Sullen. Norris played Scrub and Cibber Gibbet. Other members of the cast were Mrs Bradshaw and Mrs Bicknell, Verbruggen, Mills, and Bullock. The play was staged fifteen times, and became part of the theatre's regular repertory, as it did at Drury Lane, where it was first performed in 1708. In the next twenty-one years there were sixty-five performances in this theatre and at least twenty-five in the Haymarket. The play was first performed at Lincoln's Inn Fields in 1721; there were twenty-three performances in the period 1721–29. Quin played Sullen in the 1721 (Nov.) production, Ryan played Archer, and the younger Bullock Scrub, while his father played Bonniface, as in the first performance at the Haymarket. Mrs Bullock played Dorinda, the other actresses being Mrs Seymour, Mrs Roger and Mrs Egleton.

Among the interesting performances of the play that of 1740 in Drury Lane must be remembered, for Mills played Archer, Macklin Scrub, and Milward Aimwell; and Mrs Pritchard and Mrs Clive played Mrs Sullen and Cherry. In 1742 Garrick played Archer for the first time: it became one of his favourite parts and was a role in which Smith, Elliston, and Kemble distinguished themselves. This 1742 performance with Peg Woffington as Mrs Sullen and Macklin as Scrub must have been excellent. Garrick played Archer on several occasions, at Covent Garden (1746), and at Drury Lane (1767 and 1774) where he played Scrub in 1761. Scrub was played by Shuter (1774), Quick (1778, 1785, and 1798), Banister the Younger (1802), Dowton (1802), Liston (1810), Johnstone (1821), Keeley (1828). In 1785 Mrs Abington played Mrs Sullen in Drury Lane. She had played this role when the play was first performed in Ireland, at the Smock Alley Theatre's re-opening in Dublin (1759). Those who played Mrs Sullen included Mrs Abington (1774, 1785 and 1798), Mrs Barry (1778), Miss Farren (1779), Mrs Gordan (1802), Mrs Kemble (1810), Mrs Davison (1818), Miss Chester (1823), and Miss Litton (1879). Cherry was played notably by Mrs Clive (1740), Mrs Vincent (1746), Miss Pope (1767, 1774), Miss Brown (1774), Mrs Martyr (1785–98), Miss Millar (1802), and Mrs Gibbs (1810–19).

The play continued to be performed in the nineteenth century. There were performances in 1802, while in 1810 *The Beaux Stratagem* was staged (as a *Ballet d'action* to evade the Patent Act) at the Royal Circus. Other performances were those of 1810, 1816, 1818 (Drury Lane); 1819 (Covent Garden); 1821, 1823 (Haymarket); 1828 (Covent Garden); 1830 (Drury Lane); 1832 (Covent Garden); 1842, 1847, 1856 (all at the Haymarket); 1878 (Annexe Theatre at Westminster Aquarium); 1879 (Imperial).

Twentieth-century performances include that of 1919 (Haymarket, abridged version) with Sybil Thorndike as Cherry and Russell Thorndike as Archer, 1925 (Cambridge), 1926 (Norwich), 1927 (Lyric, Hammersmith—a heavily cut version); 1930 (Royalty) with Edith Evans as Mrs Sullen, 1947 (Intimate Theatre, Manchester), 1949 (Phoenix), and 1970 with Maggie Smith as Mrs Sullen (National).

2. *In the United States*

The Beaux Stratagem was performed in Williamsburg "by the gentlemen and ladies of this country" in 1736. It may have been performed earlier in New York in 1734 (T. Allston Brown, *History of the New York Stage*), but Professor G. C. D. Odell regards the first New York production as that given in "The new theater in the Broad-way" (probably Master Rip Van Dam's Theatre) on 12 February 1741.[14]

Performances in 1750 and 1751 were given in New York by the Murray-Kean company, the first professional actors to visit New York. In 1752 the Hallam company, which had crossed the Atlantic on the *Charming Sally*, rehearsing en route, gave a performance of *The Beaux Stratagem*, and the play was staged again on 7 Dec. 1767 for the first night of the new John Street Theatre in New York.

British officers performed many plays in this theatre during the British occupation (1777–83), including *The Beaux Stratagem* in their repertoire. On 16 Feb. 1777 they played it for the benefit of the widows and children of the Hessian soldiers, and again on 27 Feb. for the relief of the distressed inhabitants. Before the troops left, there were many performances of the play in this theatre, which was renamed the Theatre Royal.

In 1785 the Hallam company returned and again acted the play, repeating it on 14 Apr. 1789 in the John Street Theatre and on several other occasions, notably in 1793 with John Hodgkinson as Archer and Hallam as Scrub. The play was frequently performed. There were, for instance, performances in 1809 (when the Hon. Mrs Thistleton played Mrs Sullen), in 1810 and 1814 (when John Dwyer acted Archer), and 1815.

Other outstanding performances were those of 26 Nov. 1822 at the Park Theatre (with Charles Matthews as Scrub and Miss Johnson as Cherry), of 4 Nov. 1829 (with George Barret as Archer and Mrs Barnes as Mrs Sullen), and of 11 Sept. 1841 (with J. S. Browne as Archer and Charlotte Cushman as Mrs Sullen).

In the twentieth century the play does not seem to have been so popular on the professional stage though often acted in college and university theatre productions. In 1928 The Players Club revived *The Beaux Stratagem* at the Hampden Theatre in New York. There was another production at the Phoenix Theatre (opening in February 1959) and the Equity Theatre offered a production opening in March 1966.

Information on the play's stage history can be found in John Genest, *Some Account of the English Stage From the Restoration in*

---

[14] His comment is in "The Players add a Chapter to Stage Annals" in an unidentified New York newspaper, date stamped 27 May 1928, in the Theatre Collection, Harvard University Library.

1660 to 1830. 10 vols. (1832); Allardyce Nicoll, *Restoration Drama* (1923); *A History of Early Eighteenth Century Drama* (1925); and *A History of English Drama 1660—1900* I and II (1925; 1952); and in *The English Stage, 1660–1800,* Part 2, *1700–29,* ed. Emmett L. Avery (1960); Part 3, *1729–47,* ed. Arthur H. Scouten (1961); Part 4, *1747–76,* ed. George Winchester Stone (1962).

For American productions Odell's *Annals of the New York Stage* (1927–1949) provides information, and two useful articles, associated with the Players Club revival of 1928, were written by H. I. Brock, "A Comedy returns from Colonial Times", *New York Times* 3 June 1928, and by G. C. D. Odell, "The Players add a Chapter to Stage Annals" (see fn 14, p. 15). The present editor is indebted to Arnold Wengrow, the Theatre Collection of the Harvard College Library, and to Mary Ann Jensen, Curator of the Theatre Collection, Princeton University Library, for their help in tracing American productions of the play.

A NOTE ON THE TEXT

The Beaux Stratagem was initially performed on 8 March 1706/7. The first edition was published on the 27 March following, and was printed "for Bernard Lintot at the *Cross-Keys* next *Nando's* Coffee House in *Fleet street*". (Publication had been announced in the *Daily Courant* on Wednesday, 5 March 1706/7 for 8 March.[1]) No manuscript sources for the text of the play are known, but the first edition was presumably set from the author's manuscript for which Lintot paid Farquhar £30, probably as an advance, on 27 January 1706/7.[2]

As Farquhar died in May 1707, authorial intervention in the text cannot be large.[3] According to Professor Allardyce Nicoll (*A History of English Drama 1660–1900*, *II*, 3rd ed., 1952, p. 322) there are nine editions of 1707, the first of which is undated. This is incorrect but both the first and second editions of the *Cambridge Bibliography of English Literature* make the same mistake. The earliest edition is indeed undated and it is perhaps the variety of states in which its text is found that has misled Professor Nicoll. The second edition, which may readily be distinguished by the description "The Second Edition" on the title page, is also undated. This follows the first edition closely, though some corrections have been made. (An extra line is added on p. 45; p. 46 carries over an extra line; p. 47 returns to the pagination of [1707].) Because of the closeness of the second edition to the first it has seemed convenient to describe it as [1707²]. I have not been able to find any other early edition with readings that should be taken into consideration. Accordingly I have used as copy text the British Museum copy of the [1707] first edition (press mark: 11775 g. 17). This has been collated with copies of the same edition in the Brotherton Collection, University of Leeds, the National Library of Scotland, the University of Edinburgh Library, the Michigan University Library, Pembroke College, Cambridge, the Yale University Library, the Houghton

---

[1] See Professor Shirley Strum Kenny, Letter to *Times Literary Supplement*, 17 September 1971.

[2] See "Lintot's Accounts", *Literary Anecdotes of the Eighteenth Century*, ed. John Nichols, vol. VIII, p. 296. London, 1814.

[3] See Critical Introduction, p. 1.

Library, Harvard, the University of Illinois Library, and with two copies in the University of Texas Library and two copies in the Bodleian Library, Oxford. There are other copies of the first edition in the Folger Shakespeare Library; the Newberry Library, Chicago; the University of Pennsylvania Library; the Princeton University Library; and the William Andrews Clark Library, Los Angeles. It has also been collated with the copies of the second edition [1707²] in the Michigan University Library and in the Cornell University Library. There are other copies of the second edition in the Folger Shakespeare Library and in the Johns Hopkins University Library. The Textual Notes record all departures from the copy text, except for the silent corrections recorded below.

Where the present editor's emendations have been anticipated by the editors of *The Comedies of Mr. George Farquhar* [1710?] and *The Works of the late Ingenious Mr. George Farquhar: containing all his Letters, Poems, Essays and Comedies Publish'd in his Life-time* [1711] this has been recorded by way of acknowledgement. The dating of *The Comedies* as [1707] in the *Cambridge Bibliography of English Literature* is so doubtful in view of the recent dating of a copy of it in the Bodleian Library as [1709] that it has seemed wiser to deny textual authority at the present moment both to this collection of *Farquhar's Comedies*⁴ and, obviously, to the *Works*.

The British Museum contains other London editions of 1733 (the 8th edition); 1748; 1752; 1755; 1760; 1763; 1770; 1771; 1775; 1778; and 1798. Other editions listed elsewhere are those of 1710 (a copy in the William Andrews Clark Library, Los Angeles; its title page gives London as its place of printing. It is too fragile to photograph but is believed to be a copy of the impression to which the Michigan and Cornell texts belong); 1720; 1739; and 1768. There were three Edinburgh editions of 1715; and others of 1755; and 1768. An edition was published in Belfast in 1767. Dublin editions appeared in 1724; 1729; 1739; 1753; 1766; 1775; and 1792. Thomas Ewing's Dublin edition of the *Works* (1775) contained the *Life* by T. Wilkes.

The play was included in *The Comedies of Mr. George Farquhar* [1709]; [1710?]; 1711; 1714; 1721; 1728; and 1736 (the 7th edition in 2 vols, entitled *The Dramatic Works of Mr. George Farquhar*). The date of [1709] for the *Comedies* is based on that assigned to the copy in

---

⁴ See the present editor's letter to the *Times Literary Supplement* of 23 July 1971, and Professor Shirley Strum Kenny's letter already referred to.

the Bodleian Library, on the evidence of advertisements of books printed in 1708 *viz* "Mr. *Wingate's* Arithmetick . . .", "The History of the Jews . . .". The *"Oxford* and *Cambridge* Miscellenary Poems" 1708 is also advertised, as well as two volumes in Mr Foxon's catalogue: "The Art of Cookery in Imitation of Horace's Art of Poetry . . .", advertised on 8 January 1708 in the *Daily Courant*, and *The Art of Love*, advertised on 29 April 1708 in the *London Gazette*. I am indebted to Mr D. G. Neill of the Bodleian Library for this information. Professor Shirley Strum Kenny, in her letter to the *Times Literary Supplement* of 17 September 1971, dates the publication of the *Comedies* as 27 March 1708, citing the *Daily Courant*. The play was also included in *The Works of the late Ingenious Mr. George Farquhar: containing all his Letters, Poems, Essays, and Comedies Publish'd in his Life-time*, [1711]; 1711 (this is described as "The second edition" on its general title page;[5]) 1714; 1718; 1721; 1728 (6th edition); 1736 (7th edition in 2 vols); 1742 (8th edition); 1760 (9th edition); and 1772 (10th edition). It was also included in *The Dramatic Works of George Farquhar*, ed. A. C. Ewald (2 vols, 1892); in *George Farquhar*, ed. W. Archer, (4 plays, in the Mermaid Series, 1906); in *Representative English Dramas from Dryden to Sheridan*, ed. Frederick Tupper and J. W. [James Wadell] (1914); in *A Discourse upon Comedy, The Recruiting Officer and The Beaux Stratagem*, ed. Louis A. Strauss (1914); in *The Complete Works of George Farquhar*, ed. C. Stonehill (2 vols, 1930); in *British Dramatists from Dryden to Sheridan*, ed. G. H. Nettleton and A. E. Case (1939); in *Three Restoration Comedies*, ed. Norman Marshall (1953); and in *Eighteenth Century Comedy*, ed. S. Trussler (1969). The play was edited by H. M. Fitzgibbon (1898); by Bonamy Dobrée (Bristol, 1929); and by Vincent F. Hopper and Gerald B. Lahey with a Note on the Staging by George L. Hersey (New York, 1963).

In the present edition the title has been spelled throughout without an apostrophe after *Beaux* and the following silent alterations have been made. The long s has been transcribed in accordance with modern usage throughout the text. Catchwords have been abandoned, contracted names have been expanded in speech prefixes and stage directions, and the latter have been normalised. All other changes have been listed in the textual notes; those affecting meaning have been set at the foot of the text pages and all others on pp. 109–113 at the back of the book.

[5] See again the two letters to the *Times Literary Supplement* referred to above.

Both pointed and square brackets in this edition are editorial. The former enclose material supplied by the editor; the latter have been used merely to distinguish between text and original stage directions where there is any danger of confusion, *i.e.* where a direction occurs in running text and not either ranged to the side or set on a line by itself. The original square bracket of the copy text which preceded every stage direction ranged to the right, has been abolished. Where directions such as "*aside*" occur set to the right in the copy text, they have been moved so that they now precede the sentence of speech to which they refer, thus clarifying the action.

ADVERTISEMENT

The Reader may find some Faults in this Play, which my Illness prevented the amending of, but there is great Amends made in the Representation, which cannot be match'd, no more than the friendly and indefatigable Care of Mr *Wilks*, to whom I chiefly owe the Success of the Play.

GEORGE FARQUHAR.

PROLOGUE

Spoken by Mr Wilks.

When Strife disturbs or Sloth Corrupts an Age,
Keen Satyr is the Business of the Stage.
When the Plain-Dealer *writ, he lash'd those Crimes*
Which then infested most—The Modish Times:
But now, when Faction sleeps and Sloth is fled,   5
And all our Youth in Active Fields are bred;
When thro' GREAT BRITAIN'*s fair extensive Round,*
The Trumps of Fame the Notes of Union *sound;*
When ANNA'*s Scepter points the Laws their Course,*
And Her Example gives her Precepts Force: 10
There scarce is room for Satyr, all our Lays
Must be, or Songs of Triumph, or of Praise:
But as in Grounds best cultivated, Tares
And Poppies rise among the Golden Ears;
Our Products so, fit for the Field or School,   15
Must mix with Nature's Favourite Plant—A Fool:
A Weed that has to twenty Summers ran,
Shoots up in Stalk, and Vegetates to Man.
Simpling our Author goes from Field to Field,
And culls such Fools, as may Diversion yield;   20
And, Thanks to Nature, there's no want of those,
For Rain, or Shine, the thriving Coxcomb grows.
Follies, to Night we shew, ne'er lash'd before,
Yet, such as Nature shews you every Hour;
Nor can the Pictures give a Just Offence,   25
For Fools are made for Jests to Men of Sense.

DRAMATIS PERSONAE

MEN

AIMWELL, ARCHER,	*Two Gentlemen of broken Fortunes, the first as Master, and the second as Servant.*	Mr Mills. Mr Wilks.
COUNT BELLAIR,	*A French Officer, Prisoner at Litchfield.*	Mr Bowman.
SULLEN,	*A Country Blockhead, brutal to his Wife.*	Mr Verbruggen.
FREEMAN,	*A Gentleman from London.*	Mr Keen.
FOIGARD,	*A Priest, Chaplain to the French Officers.*	Mr Bowen.
GIBBET,	*A High-way-man.*	Mr Cibber.
HOUNSLOW, BAGSHOT,	*His Companions.*	
BONNIFACE,	*Landlord of the Inn.*	Mr Bullock.
SCRUB,	*Servant to Mr Sullen.*	Mr Norris.
⟨A FELLOW,	*Messenger.*⟩	

WOMEN

LADY BOUNTIFUL,	*An old civil Country Gentlewoman, that cures all her Neighbours of all Distempers, and foolishly fond of her Son Sullen.*	Mrs Powel.
DORINDA	*Lady Bountiful's Daughter.*	Mrs Bradshaw.

MRS SULLEN,	*Her Daughter-in-law.*	Mrs Oldfield.
GIPSEY,	*Maid to the Ladies.*	Mrs Mills.
CHERRY,	*The Landlord's Daughter in the Inn.*	Mrs Bignal.

⟨COUNTRY WOMAN⟩

SCENE, *Litchfield*

ACT I

SCENE I

SCENE, *an Inn.*

Enter BONNIFACE *running.*

BONNIFACE. Chamberlain, Maid, *Cherry*, Daughter *Cherry*, all
asleep, all dead?

Enter CHERRY *running.*

CHERRY. Here, here, Why d'ye baul so, Father? dy'e think we
have no Ears?

BONNIFACE. You deserve to have none, you young Minx;—The   5
Company of the *Warrington* Coach has stood in the Hall this
Hour, and no Body to shew them to their Chambers.

CHERRY. And let 'em wait farther; there's neither Red-Coat in
the Coach, nor Footman behind it.

BONNIFACE. But they threaten to go to another Inn to Night.   10

CHERRY. That they dare not, for fear the Coachman should
overturn them to Morrow—Coming, coming: Here's the *London*
Coach arriv'd.

*Enter several People with Trunks, Band-boxes, and other Luggage,
and cross the Stage.*

BONNIFACE. Welcome, Ladies.

CHERRY. Very welcome, Gentlemen—Chamberlain, shew the   15
Lyon and the *Rose.*

Exit with the Company.

Enter AIMWELL *in riding Habit,* ARCHER *as Footman carrying a
Portmantle.*

BONNIFACE. This way, this way, Gentlemen.

AIMWELL. Set down the things, go to the Stable, and see my
Horses well rubb'd.

B

ARCHER. I shall, Sir.   20

Exit.

AIMWELL. You're my Landlord, I suppose?

BONNIFACE. Yes, Sir, I'm old *Will. Bonniface*, pretty well known
upon this Road, as the saying is.

AIMWELL. O Mr. *Bonniface*, your Servant.

BONNIFACE. O Sir—What will your Honour please to drink,   25
as the saying is?

AIMWELL. I have heard your Town of *Litchfield* much fam'd for
Ale, I think I'll taste that.

BONNIFACE. Sir, I have now in my Cellar Ten Tun of the best
Ale in *Staffordshire*; 'tis smooth as Oil, sweet as Milk, clear as   30
Amber, and strong as Brandy; and will be just Fourteen Year old
the Fifth Day of next *March* old Stile.

AIMWELL. You're very exact, I find, in the Age of your Ale.

BONNIFACE. As punctual, Sir, as I am in the Age of my Children:
I'll shew you such Ale—Here, Tapster, broach Number 1706,   35
as the saying is;—Sir, you shall taste my *Anno Domini*;—I have
liv'd in *Litchfield* Man and Boy above Eight and fifty Years, and I
believe have not consum'd Eight and fifty Ounces of Meat.

AIMWELL. At a Meal, you mean, if one may guess your Sense by
your Bulk.   40

BONNIFACE. Not in my Life, Sir, I have fed purely upon Ale;
I have eat my Ale, drank my Ale, and I always sleep upon Ale.

Enter Tapster with a Bottle and Glass.

Now, Sir, you shall see [*filling it out*] your Worship's Health;
ha! delicious, delicious,—fancy it *Burgundy*, only fancy it, and
'tis worth Ten Shillings a Quart.   45

AIMWELL. [*Drinks*] 'Tis confounded strong.

BONNIFACE. Strong! It must be so, or how should we be strong
that drink it?

AIMWELL. And have you liv'd so long upon this Ale, Landlord?

BONNIFACE. Eight and fifty Years, upon my Credit, Sir; but it   50
kill'd my Wife, poor Woman, as the saying is.

AIMWELL. How came that to pass?

BONNIFACE. I don't know how, Sir; she would not let the Ale
take its natural Course, Sir, she was for qualifying it every now
and then with a Dram, as the saying is; and an honest Gentleman 55

that came this way from *Ireland*, made her a Present of a dozen
Bottles of Usquebaugh—But the poor Woman was never well
after: But howe're, I was obliged to the Gentleman, you know.

AIMWELL. Why, was it the Usquebaugh that kill'd her?

BONNIFACE. My Lady *Bountiful* said so,—She, good Lady, did 60
what could be done, she cured her of Three Tympanies, but the
Fourth carry'd her off; but she's happy, and I'm contented, as the
saying is.

AIMWELL. Who's that Lady *Bountiful*, you mention'd?

BONNIFACE. Ods my Life, Sir, we'll drink her Health. [*Drinks*] 65
My Lady *Bountiful* is one of the best of Women: Her last Husband
Sir *Charles Bountiful* left her worth a Thousand Pound a Year;
and I believe she lays out one half on't in charitable Uses for the
Good of her Neighbours; she cures Rheumatisms, Ruptures, and
broken Shins in Men, Green Sickness, Obstructions, and Fits of 70
the Mother in Women;—The Kings-Evil, Chin-Cough, and
Chilblains in Children; in short, she has cured more People in
and about *Litchfield* within Ten Years than the Doctors have
kill'd in Twenty; and that's a bold Word.

AIMWELL. Has the Lady been any other way useful in her Genera- 75
tion?

BONNIFACE. Yes, Sir, She has a Daughter by Sir *Charles*, the
finest Woman in all our Country, and the greatest Fortune. She
has a Son too by her first Husband Squire *Sullen*, who marry'd a
fine Lady from *London* t'other Day; if you please, Sir, we'll drink 80
his Health?

AIMWELL. What sort of a Man is he?

BONNIFACE. Why, Sir, the Man's well enough; says little, thinks
less, and does—nothing at all, Faith: But he's a Man of a great
Estate, and values no Body. 85

AIMWELL. A Sportsman, I suppose.

BONNIFACE. Yes, Sir, he's a Man of Pleasure, he plays at Whisk,
and smoaks his Pipe Eight and forty Hours together sometimes.

AIMWELL. And marry'd, you say?

BONNIFACE. Ay, and to a curious Woman, Sir,—But he's a—He 90
wants it, here, Sir.

Pointing to his Forehead.

AIMWELL. He has it there, you mean.

BONNIFACE. That's none of my Business, he's my Landlord,

and so a Man you know, wou'd not,—But—I cod, he's no
better than—Sir, my humble Service to you. [*Drinks.*] Tho' I   95
value not a Farthing what he can do to me; I pay him his Rent
at Quarter day, I have a good running Trade, I have but one
Daughter, and I can give her—But no matter for that.

AIMWELL. You're very happy, Mr *Bonniface*, pray what other
Company have you in Town?   100

BONNIFACE. A power of fine Ladies, and then we have the *French*
Officers.

AIMWELL. O that's right, you have a good many of those Gentlemen: Pray how do you like their Company?

BONNIFACE. So well, as the saying is, that I cou'd wish we had as   105
many more of 'em, they're full of Money, and pay double for
every thing they have; they know, Sir, that we pay'd good
round Taxes for the taking of 'em, and so they are willing to
reimburse us a little; one of 'em lodges in my House.

Enter ARCHER.

ARCHER. Landlord, there are some *French* Gentlemen below   110
that ask for you.

BONNIFACE. I'll wait on 'em;—Does your Master stay long in
Town, as the saying is?

To ARCHER.

ARCHER. I can't tell, as the saying is.

BONNIFACE. Come from *London*?   115

ARCHER. No.

BONNIFACE. Going to *London*, may hap?

ARCHER. No.

BONNIFACE. An odd Fellow this. I beg your Worship's
Pardon, I'll wait on you in half a Minute.   120

Exit.

AIMWELL. The Coast's clear, I see,—Now my dear *Archer*, welcome to *Litchfield*.

ARCHER. I thank thee, my dear Brother in Iniquity.

AIMWELL. Iniquity! prithee leave Canting, you need not change
your Stile with your Dress.   125

ARCHER. Don't mistake me, *Aimwell*, for 'tis still my Maxim,
that there is no Scandal like Rags, nor any Crime so shameful
as Poverty.

AIMWELL. The World confesses it every Day in its Practice, tho'
Men won't own it for their Opinion: Who did that worthy 130
Lord, my Brother, single out of the Side-box to sup with him
t'other Night?

ARCHER. *Jack Handycraft*, a handsom, well dress'd, mannerly,
sharping Rogue, who keeps the best Company in Town.

AIMWELL. Right, and pray who marry'd my Lady *Man-* 135
slaughter t'other Day, the great Fortune?

ARCHER. Why, *Nick Marrabone*, a profess'd Pick-pocket, and
a good Bowler; but he makes a handsom Figure, and rides in his
Coach, that he formerly used to ride behind.

AIMWELL. But did you observe poor *Jack Generous* in the Park 140
last Week?

ARCHER. Yes, with his Autumnal Perriwig, shading his melancholly Face, his Coat older than any thing but its Fashion, with
one Hand idle in his Pocket, and with the other picking his useless Teeth; and tho' the Mall was crowded with Company, yet 145
was poor *Jack* as single and solitary as a Lyon in a Desart.

AIMWELL. And as much avoided, for no Crime upon Earth but
the want of Money.

ARCHER. And that's enough; Men must not be poor, Idleness is
the Root of all Evil; the World's wide enough, let 'em bustle; 150
Fortune has taken the weak under her Protection, but Men of
Sense are left to their Industry.

AIMWELL. Upon which Topick we proceed, and I think luckily
hitherto: Wou'd not any Man swear now that I am a Man of
Quality, and you my Servant, when if our intrinsick Value were 155
known—

ARCHER. Come, come, we are the Men of intrinsick Value, who
can strike our Fortunes out of our selves, whose worth is indepen-
dent of Accidents in Life, or Revolutions in Government; we
have Heads to get Money, and Hearts to spend it.   160

AIMWELL. As to our Hearts, I grant'ye, they are as willing Tits
as any within Twenty Degrees; but I can have no great opinion
of our Heads from the Service they have done us hitherto, unless
it be that they have brought us from *London* hither to *Litchfield*,
made me a Lord, and you my Servant.   165

ARCHER. That's more than you cou'd expect already. But what
Money have we left?

AIMWELL. But Two hundred Pound.

ARCHER. And our Horses, Cloaths, Rings, etc. why we have very
good Fortunes now for moderate People; and let me tell you,   170
besides, that this Two hundred Pound, with the experience that
we are now Masters of, is a better Estate than the Ten Thousand
we have spent.—Our Friends indeed began to suspect that our
Pockets were low; but we came off with flying Colours, shew'd
no signs of want either in Word or Deed.   175

AIMWELL. Ay, and our going to *Brussels* was a good Pretence
enough for our sudden disappearing; and I warrant you, our
Friends imagine that we are gone a volunteering.

ARCHER. Why Faith, if this Prospect fails, it must e'en come to
that, I am for venturing one of the Hundreds if you will upon this   180
Knight-Errantry; but in case it should fail, we'll reserve the
t'other to carry us to some Counterscarp, where we may die as we
liv'd in a Blaze.

AIMWELL. With all my Heart; and we have liv'd justly, *Archer*,
we can't say that we have spent our Fortunes, but that we have   185
enjoy'd 'em.

ARCHER. Right, so much Pleasure for so much Money, we have
had our Penyworths, and had I Millions, I wou'd go to the same
Market again. O *London, London*! well, we have had our share,
and let us be thankful; Past Pleasures, for ought I know are   190
best, such as we are sure of, those to come may disappoint us.

AIMWELL. It has often griev'd the Heart of me, to see how some
inhumane Wretches murther their kind Fortunes; those that by
sacrificing all to one Appetite, shall starve all the rest.—You
shall have some that live only in their Palates, and in their sense of   195
tasting shall drown the other Four: Others are only Epicures in
Appearances, such who shall starve their Nights to make a Figure
a Days, and famish their own to feed the Eyes of others: A
contrary Sort confine their Pleasures to the dark, and contract
their spacious Acres to the Circuit of a Muff-string.   200

ARCHER. Right; but they find the *Indies* in that Spot where they
consume 'em, and I think your kind Keepers have much the best
on't; for they indulge the most Senses by one Expence, there's
the Seeing, Hearing, and Feeling amply gratify'd; and some

170–1. you, besides, that] s; you, besides Thousand, that 1707, 1707²; you, that,
172–3. Ten Thousand we] s; Ten we 1707, 1707².

Philosophers will tell you, that from such a Commerce there 205
arises a sixth Sense that gives infinitely more Pleasure than the
other five put together.

AIMWELL. And to pass to the other Extremity, of all Keepers, I
think those the worst that keep their Money.

ARCHER. Those are the most miserable Wights in being, they 210
destroy the Rights of Nature, and disappoint the Blessings of
Providence: Give me a Man that keeps his Five Senses keen and
bright as his Sword, that has 'em always drawn out in their just
order and strength, with his Reason as Commander at the
Head of 'em, that detaches 'em by turns upon whatever Party of 215
Pleasure agreeably offers, and commands 'em to retreat upon the
least Appearance of Disadvantage or Danger:—For my part I can
stick to my Bottle, while my Wine, my Company, and my
Reason holds good; I can be charm'd with *Sappho's* singing
without falling in Love with her Face; I love Hunting, but wou'd 220
not, like *Acteon*, be eaten up by my own Dogs; I love a fine
House, but let another keep it; and just so I love a fine Woman.

AIMWELL. In that last particular you have the better of me.

ARCHER. Ay, you're such an amorous Puppy, that I'm afraid
you'll spoil our Sport; you can't counterfeit the Passion with- 225
out feeling it.

AIMWELL. Tho' the whining part be out of doors in Town, 'tis
still in force with the Country Ladies;—And let me tell you
Frank, the Fool in that Passion shall outdoe the Knave at any
time. 230

ARCHER. Well, I won't dispute it now, you Command for the
Day, and so I submit;—At *Nottingham* you know I am to be
Master.

AIMWELL. And at *Lincoln* I again.

ARCHER. Then at *Norwich* I mount, which, I think, shall be our 235
last Stage; for if we fail there, we'll imbark for *Holland*, bid
adieu to *Venus*, and welcome *Mars*.

AIMWELL. A Match! [*Enter* BONNIFACE.] Mum.

BONNIFACE. What will your Worship please to have for
Supper? 240

AIMWELL. What have you got?

BONNIFACE. Sir, we have a delicate piece of Beef in the Pot, and
a Pig at the Fire.

AIMWELL. Good Supper-meat, I must confess,—I can't eat Beef, Landlord.   245

ARCHER. And I hate Pig.

AIMWELL. Hold your prating, Sirrah, do you know who you are?

BONNIFACE. Please to bespeak something else, I have every thing in the House.

AIMWELL. Have you any Veal?   250

BONNIFACE. Veal! Sir, we had a delicate Loin of Veal on *Wednesday* last.

AIMWELL. Have you got any Fish or Wildfowl?

BONNIFACE. As for Fish, truly Sir, we are an inland Town, and indifferently provided with Fish, that's the Truth on't, and then   255
for Wildfowl,—We have a delicate Couple of Rabbets.

AIMWELL. Get me the Rabbets fricasy'd.

BONNIFACE. Fricasy'd! Lard, Sir, they'll eat much better smother'd with Onions.

ARCHER. Pshaw! damn your Onions.   260

AIMWELL. Again, Sirrah!—Well, Landlord, what you please; but hold, I have a small Charge of Money, and your House is so full of Strangers, that I believe it may be safer in your Custody than mine; for when this Fellow of mine gets drunk, he minds nothing.—Here, Sirrah, reach me the strong Box.   265

ARCHER. Yes, Sir.—[*Aside.*] This will give us a Reputation.

Brings the Box.

AIMWELL. Here, Landlord, the Locks are sealed down both for your Security and mine; it holds somewhat above Two hundred Pound; if you doubt it, I'll count it to you after Supper; but be sure you lay it where I may have it at a Minute's warning; for my   270
Affairs are a little dubious at present, perhaps I may be gone in half an Hour, perhaps I may be your Guest till the best part of that be spent; and pray order your Ostler to keep my Horses always sadled; but one thing above the rest I must beg, that you would let this Fellow have none of your *Anno Domini*, as you   275
call it;—For he's the most insufferable Sot—Here, Sirrah, light me to my Chamber.

Exit lighted by ARCHER.

BONNIFACE. *Cherry*, Daughter *Cherry*?

Enter CHERRY.

CHERRY. D'ye call, Father?

BONNIFACE. Ay, Child, you must lay by this Box for the 280
Gentleman, 'tis full of Money.

CHERRY. Money! all that Money! why, sure Father the Gentleman comes to be chosen Parliament-man. Who is he?

BONNIFACE. I don't know what to make of him, he talks of
keeping his Horses ready sadled, and of going perhaps at a 285
minute's warning, or of staying perhaps till the best part of this
be spent.

CHERRY. Ay, ten to one, Father, he's a High-way-man.

BONNIFACE. A High-way-man! upon my Life, Girl, you have
hit it, and this Box is some new purchased Booty.—Now 290
cou'd we find him out, the Money were ours.

CHERRY. He don't belong to our Gang.

BONNIFACE. What Horses have they?

CHERRY. The Master rides upon a Black.

BONNIFACE. A Black! ten to one the Man upon the black Mare; 295
and since he don't belong to our Fraternity, we may betray him
with a safe Conscience; I don't think it lawful to harbour any
Rogues but my own.—Look'ye, Child, as the saying is, we must
go cunningly to work, Proofs we must have, the Gentleman's
Servant loves Drink, I'll ply him that way, and ten to one loves a 300
Wench; you must work him t'other way.

CHERRY. Father, wou'd you have me give my Secret for his?

BONNIFACE. Consider, Child, there's Two hundred Pound to
Boot. [*Ringing without.*] Coming, coming.—Child, mind your
Business.   305

CHERRY. What a Rogue is my Father! my Father! I deny it.—
My Mother was a good, generous, free-hearted Woman, and I
can't tell how far her good Nature might have extended for the
good of her Children. This Landlord of mine, for I think I can
call him no more, would betray his Guest, and debauch his 310
Daughter into the bargain,—By a Footman too!

Enter ARCHER.

ARCHER. What Footman, pray, Mistress, is so happy as to be the
Subject of your Contemplation?

CHERRY. Whoever he is, Friend, he'll be but little the better for't.

ARCHER. I hope so, for I'm sure you did not think of me.   315

CHERRY.   Suppose I had?

ARCHER.   Why then you're but even with me; for the Minute I
came in, I was a considering in what manner I should make love
to you.

CHERRY.   Love to me, Friend!   320

ARCHER.   Yes, Child.

CHERRY.   Child! Manners; if you kept a little more distance,
Friend, it would become you much better.

ARCHER.   Distance! good night, Sauce-box.

Going.

CHERRY.   A pretty Fellow! I like his Pride,—Sir, pray, Sir, you   325
see, Sir, [ARCHER *returns*] I have the Credit to be intrusted
with your Master's Fortune here, which sets me a Degree above
his Footman; I hope, Sir, you an't affronted.

ARCHER.   Let me look you full in the Face, and I'll tell you
whether you can affront me or no.—S'death, Child, you have a   330
pair of delicate Eyes, and you don't know what to do with 'em.

CHERRY.   Why, Sir, don't I see every body?

ARCHER.   Ay, but if some Women had 'em, they wou'd kill
every body.—Prithee, instruct me, I wou'd fain make Love to
you, but I don't know what to say.   335

CHERRY.   Why, did you never make Love to any body before?

ARCHER.   Never to a Person of your Figure, I can assure you,
Madam, my Addresses have been always confin'd to People within
my own Sphere, I never aspir'd so high before.

> But you look so bright,   340
> And are dress'd so tight,
> That a Man wou'd swear you're Right,
> As Arm was e'er laid over.

> Such an Air
> You freely wear   345
> To ensnare
> As makes each Guest a Lover.

> Since then, my Dear, I'm your Guest,
> Prithee give me of the Best

340. But you look . . .] The full text of the song is taken from *The Dramaitck
Works* (1736); the first two lines only are given in 1707, 1707², c, w.

Of what is ready Drest: 350
Since then my Dear etc.

A Song.

CHERRY. [*Aside.*] What can I think of this Man? Will you give
me that Song, Sir?

ARCHER. Ay, my Dear, take it while 'tis warm. [*Kisses her.*]
Death and Fire! her Lips are Honey-combs.   355

CHERRY. And I wish there had been Bees too, to have stung you
for your Impudence.

ARCHER. There's a swarm of *Cupids*, my little *Venus*, that has
done the Business much better.

CHERRY. [*Aside.*] This Fellow is misbegotten as well as I. 360
What's your Name, Sir?

ARCHER. [*Aside.*] Name! I gad, I have forgot it. Oh! *Martin*.

CHERRY. Where were you born?

ARCHER. In St *Martin's* Parish.

CHERRY. What was your Father?   365

ARCHER. St *Martin's* Parish.

CHERRY. Then, Friend, good night.

ARCHER. I hope not.

CHERRY. You may depend upon't.

ARCHER. Upon what?   370

CHERRY. That's you're very impudent.

ARCHER. That you're very handsome.

CHERRY. That you're a Footman.

ARCHER. That you're an Angel.

CHERRY. I shall be rude.   375

ARCHER. So shall I.

CHERRY. Let go my Hand.

ARCHER. Give me a Kiss.

Kisses her.

Call without, Cherry, Cherry.

CHERRY. I'mm—My Father calls; you plaguy Devil, how durst 380
you stop my Breath so?—Offer to follow me one step, if you dare.

⟨*Exit* CHERRY.⟩

ARCHER. A fair Challenge by this Light; this is a pretty fair

opening of an Adventure; but we are Knight-Errants, and so
Fortune be our Guide.

Exit.

The End of the First Act

ACT II

⟨SCENE I⟩

SCENE, *A Gallery in* LADY BOUNTIFUL'S *House.*

MRS SULLEN *and* DORINDA *meeting.*

DORINDA. Morrow, my dear Sister; are you for Church this
Morning?

MRS SULLEN. Any where to Pray; for Heaven alone can help
me: But, I think, *Dorinda*, there's no Form of Prayer in the
Liturgy against bad Husbands.   5

DORINDA. But there's a Form of Law in *Doctors-Commons*; and
I swear, Sister *Sullen*, rather than see you thus continually discontented, I would advise you to apply to that: For besides the
part that I bear in your vexatious Broils, as being Sister to the
Husband, and Friend to the Wife; your Example gives me such   10
an Impression of Matrimony, that I shall be apt to condemn my
Person to a long Vacation all its Life.—But supposing, Madam,
that you brought it to a Case of Separation, what can you urge
against your Husband? My Brother is, first, the most constant
Man alive.   15

MRS SULLEN. The most constant Husband, I grant'ye.

DORINDA. He never sleeps from you.

MRS SULLEN. No, he always sleeps with me.

DORINDA. He allows you a Maintenance suitable to your
Quality.   20

MRS SULLEN. A Maintenance! do you take me, Madam, for an
hospital Child, that I must sit down, and bless my Benefactors
for Meat, Drink and Clothes? As I take it, Madam, I brought
your Brother Ten thousand Pounds, out of which, I might expect
some pretty things, call'd Pleasures.   25

DORINDA. You share in all the Pleasures that the Country affords.

MRS SULLEN. Country Pleasures! Racks and Torments! dost think, Child, that my Limbs were made for leaping of Ditches, and clambring over Stiles; or that my Parents wisely foreseeing my   30
future Happiness in Country-pleasures, had early instructed me in the rural Accomplishments of drinking fat Ale, playing at Whisk, and smoaking Tobacco with my Husband; or of spreading of Plaisters, brewing of Diet-drinks, and stilling Rosemary-Water with the good old Gentlewoman, my Mother-in-Law.   35

DORINDA. I'm sorry, Madam, that it is not more in our power to divert you; I cou'd wish indeed that our Entertainments were a little more polite, or your Taste a little less refin'd: But, pray, Madam, how came the Poets and Philosophers that labour'd so much in hunting after Pleasure, to place it at last in a Country   40
Life?

MRS SULLEN. Because they wanted Money, Child, to find out the Pleasures of the Town: Did you ever see a Poet or Philosopher worth Ten thousand Pound; if you can shew me such a Man, I'll lay you Fifty Pound you'll find him somewhere   45
within the weekly Bills.—Not that I disapprove rural Pleasures, as the Poets have painted them; in their Landschape every *Phillis* has her *Coridon*, every murmuring Stream, and every flowry Mead gives fresh Alarms to Love.—Besides, you'll find, that their Couples were never marry'd:—But yonder I see my   50
Coridon, and a sweet Swain it is, Heaven knows.—Come, *Dorinda*, don't be angry, he's my Husband, and your Brother; and between both is he not a sad Brute?

DORINDA. I have nothing to say to your part of him, you're the best Judge.   55

MRS SULLEN. O Sister, Sister! if ever you marry, beware of a sullen, silent Sot, one that's always musing, but never thinks:—There's some Diversion in a talking Blockhead; and since a Woman must wear Chains, I wou'd have the Pleasure of hearing 'em rattle a little.—Now you shall see, but take this by the way;—   60
He came home this Morning at his usual Hour of Four, waken'd me out of a sweet Dream of something else, by tumbling over the Tea-table, which be broke all to pieces, after his Man and he had rowl'd about the Room like sick Passengers in a Storm,

he comes flounce into Bed, dead as a Salmon into a Fishmonger's 65
Basket; his Feet cold as Ice, his Breath hot as a Furnace, and his
Hands and his Face as greasy as his Flanel Night-cap.—Oh
Matrimony!—He tosses up the Clothes with a barbarous swing
over his Shoulders, disorders the whole Oeconomy of my Bed,
leaves me half naked, and my whole Night's Comfort is the 70
tuneable Serenade of that wakeful Nightingale, his Nose.—O
the Pleasure of counting the melancholly Clock by a snoring
Husband!—But now, Sister, you shall see how handsomely,
being a well-bred Man, he will beg my Pardon.

Enter SULLEN.

SULLEN. My Head akes consumedly. 75
MRS SULLEN. Will you be pleased, my Dear, to drink Tea with
us this Morning? it may do your Head good.
SULLEN. No.
DORINDA. Coffee? Brother.
SULLEN. Pshaw. 80
MRS SULLEN. Will you please to dress and go to Church with
me, the Air may help you.
SULLEN. *Scrub.*

Enter SCRUB.

SCRUB. Sir.
SULLEN. What Day o'th Week is this? 85
SCRUB. *Sunday,* an't please your Worship.
SULLEN. *Sunday*! bring me a Dram, and d'ye hear, set out the
Venison-Pasty, and a Tankard of strong Beer upon the Hall-
Table, I'll go to breakfast.

Going.

DORINDA. Stay, stay, Brother, you shan't get off so; you were 90
very naughty last Night, and must make your Wife Reparation;
come, come, Brother, won't you ask Pardon?
SULLEN. For what?
DORINDA. For being drunk last Night.
SULLEN. I can afford it, can't I? 95
MRS SULLEN. But I can't, Sir.
SULLEN. Then you may let it alone.

MRS SULLEN. But I must tell you, Sir, that this is not to be born.

SULLEN. I'm glad on't.

MRS SULLEN. What is the Reason, Sir, that you use me thus   100
inhumanely?

SULLEN. *Scrub*?

SCRUB. Sir.

SULLEN. Get things ready to shave my Head.

Exit.

MRS SULLEN. Have a care of coming near his Temples, *Scrub*,   105
for fear you meet something there that may turn the Edge of your
Razor.—Inveterate Stupidity! did you ever know so hard, so
obstinate a Spleen as his? O Sister, Sister! I shall never ha'
Good of the Beast till I get him to Town; *London*, dear *London*
is the Place for managing and breaking a Husband.   110

DORINDA. And has not a Husband the same Opportunities there
for humbling a Wife?

MRS SULLEN. No, no, Child, 'tis a standing Maxim in conjugal
Discipline, that when a Man wou'd enslave his Wife, he hurries
her into the Country; and when a Lady would be arbitrary with   115
her Husband, she wheedles her Booby up to Town.—A Man
dare not play the Tyrant in *London*, because there are so many
Examples to encourage the Subject to rebel. O *Dorinda*,
Dorinda! a fine Woman may do any thing in *London*: O'my
Conscience, she may raise an Army of Forty thousand Men.   120

DORINDA. I fancy, Sister, you have a mind to be trying your
Power that way here in *Litchfield*; you have drawn the *French*
Count to your Colours already.

MRS SULLEN. The *French* are a People that can't live without
their Gallantries.   125

DORINDA. And some *English* that I know, Sister, are not averse
to such Amusements.

MRS SULLEN. Well, Sister, since the Truth must out, it may do
as well now as hereafter; I think one way to rouse my Lethargick
sotish Husband, is, to give him a Rival; Security begets Negli- 130
gence in all People, and Men must be alarm'd to make 'em alert
in their Duty: Women are like Pictures of no Value in the
Hands of a Fool, till he hears Men of Sense bid high for the
Purchase.

DORINDA. This might do, Sister, if my Brother's Understanding 135
were to be convinc'd into a Passion for you; but I fancy there's a
natural Aversion of his side; and I fancy, Sister, that you don't
come much behind him, if you dealt fairly.

MRS SULLEN. I own it, we are united Contradictions, Fire and
Water: But I cou'd be contented, with a great many other Wives, 140
to humour the censorious Mob, and give the World an Appearance of living well with my Husband, cou'd I bring him but to
dissemble a little Kindness to keep me in Countenance.

DORINDA. But how do you know, Sister, but that instead of
rousing your Husband by this Artifice to a counterfeit Kindness, 145
he should awake in a real Fury.

MRS SULLEN. Let him:—If I can't entice him to the one, I
wou'd provoke him to the other.

DORINDA. But how must I behave my self between ye.

MRS SULLEN. You must assist me. 150

DORINDA. What, against my own Brother!

MRS SULLEN. He's but half a Brother, and I'm your entire
Friend: If I go a step beyond the Bounds of Honour, leave me;
till then I expect you should go along with me in every thing,
while I trust my Honour in your Hands, you may trust your 155
Brother's in mine.—The Count is to dine here to Day.

DORINDA. 'Tis a strange thing, Sister, that I can't like that Man.

MRS SULLEN. You like nothing, your time is not come; Love
and Death have their Fatalities, and strike home one time or other:
—You'll pay for all one Day, I warrant'ye.—But, come, my 160
Lady's Tea is ready, and 'tis almost Church-time.

Exeunt.

⟨SCENE II⟩

SCENE, *The Inn.*

Enter AIMWELL *dress'd, and* ARCHER.

AIMWELL. And was she the Daughter of the House?

ARCHER. The Landlord is so blind as to think so; but I dare
swear she has better Blood in her Veins.

AIMWELL. Why dost think so?

ARCHER. Because the Baggage has a pert *Je ne scai quoi*, she   5
reads Plays, keeps a Monkey, and is troubled with Vapours.

AIMWELL. By which Discoveries I guess that you know more of
her.

ARCHER. Not yet, Faith, the Lady gives her self Airs, forsooth,
nothing under a Gentleman.   10

AIMWELL. Let me take her in hand.

ARCHER. Say one Word more o'that, and I'll declare my self,
spoil your Sport there, and every where else; look'ye, *Aimwell*,
every Man in his own Sphere.

AIMWELL. Right; and therefore you must pimp for your Master.   15

ARCHER. In the usual Forms, good Sir, after I have serv'd my
self.—But to our Business:—You are so well dress'd, *Tom*, and
make so handsome a Figure, that I fancy you may do Execution
in a Country Church; the exteriour part strikes first, and you're
in the right to make that Impression favourable.   20

AIMWELL. There's something in that which may turn to Advan-
tage: The Appearance of a Stranger in a Country Church draws
as many Gazers as a blazing Star; no sooner he comes into the
Cathedral, but a Train of Whispers runs buzzing round the
Congregation in a moment;—Who is he? whence comes he? do   25
you know him?—Then I, Sir, tips me the Verger with half a
Crown; he pockets the Simony, and Inducts me into the best
Pue in the Church, I pull out my Snuff-box, turn my self round,
bow to the Bishop, or the Dean, if he be the commanding Officer;
single out a Beauty, rivet both my Eyes to hers, set my Nose a   35
bleeding by the Strength of Imagination, and shew the whole
Church my concern by my endeavouring to hide it; after the
Sermon, the whole Town gives me to her for a Lover, and by
perswading the Lady that I am a dying for her, the Tables are
turn'd, and she in good earnest falls in Love with me?   35

ARCHER. There's nothing in this, *Tom*, without a Precedent; but
instead of riveting your Eyes to a Beauty, try to fix 'em upon a
Fortune, that's our Business at present.

AIMWELL. Pshaw, no Woman can be a Beauty without a Fortune.
—Let me alone, for I am a Mark'sman.   40

ARCHER. *Tom*.

AIMWELL. Ay.

ARCHER. When were you at Church before, pray?

AIMWELL. Um—I was there at the Coronation.

ARCHER. And how can you expect a Blessing by going to   45
Church now?

AIMWELL. Blessing! nay, *Frank*, I ask but for a Wife.

Exit.

ARCHER. Truly the Man is not very unreasonable in his Demands.

Exit at the opposite Door.

Enter BONNIFACE *and* CHERRY.

BONNIFACE. Well Daughter, as the saying is, have you brought
Martin to confess?   50

CHERRY. Pray, Father, don't put me upon getting any thing out
of a Man; I'm but young you know, Father, and I don't understand Wheedling.

BONNIFACE. Young! why you Jade, as the saying is, can any
Woman wheedle that is not young, you'r Mother was useless at   55
five and twenty; not wheedle! would you make your Mother a
Whore and me a Cuckold, as the saying is? I tell you his Silence
confesses it, and his Master spends his Money so freely, and is so
much a Gentleman every manner of way that he must be a
Highwayman.   60

Enter GIBBET *in a Cloak.*

GIBBET. Landlord, Landlord, is the Coast clear?

BONNIFACE. O, Mr *Gibbet*, what's the News?

GIBBET. No matter, ask no Questions, all fair and honourable,
here, my dear *Cherry* ⟨*Gives her a Bag.*⟩ Two hundred Sterling
Pounds as good as any that ever hang'd or sav'd a Rogue; lay 'em   65
by with the rest, and here—Three wedding or mourning Rings,
'tis much the same you know—Here, two Silver-hilted Swords;
I took those from Fellows that never shew any part of their
Swords but the Hilts: Here is a Diamond Necklace which the
Lady hid in the privatest place in the Coach, but I found it out: 70
This Gold Watch I took from a Pawn-broker's Wife; it was left
in her Hands by a Person of Quality, there's the Arms upon the
Case.

CHERRY. But who had you the Money from?

GIBBET. Ah! poor Woman! I pitied her;—From a poor Lady   75

just elop'd from her Husband, she had made up her Cargo, and
was bound for *Ireland*, as hard as she cou'd drive; she told me of
her Husband's barbarous Usage, and so I left her half a Crown:
But I had almost forgot, my dear *Cherry*, I have a Present for
you.   80

CHERRY. What is't?

GIBBET. A Pot of Cereuse, my Child, that I took out of a Lady's
under Pocket.

CHERRY. What, Mr *Gibbet*, do you think that I paint?

GIBBET. Why, you Jade, your Betters do; I'm sure the Lady   85
that I took it from had a Coronet upon her Handerchief.—Here,
take my Cloak, and go, secure the Premisses.

CHERRY. I will secure 'em.

                                                              Exit.

BONNIFACE. But, heark'ye, where's *Hounslow* and *Bagshot?*

GIBBET. They'll be here to Night.   90

BONNIFACE. D'ye know of any other Gentlemen o'the Pad on
this Road?

GIBBET. No.

BONNIFACE. I fancy that I have two that lodge in the House just
now.   95

GIBBET. The Devil! how d'ye smoak 'em?

BONNIFACE. Why, the one is gone to Church.

GIBBET. That's suspitious, I must confess.

BONNIFACE. And the other is now in his Master's Chamber;
he pretends to be Servant to the other, we'll call him out, and 100
pump him a little.

GIBBET. With all my Heart.

BONNIFACE. Mr *Martin*, Mr *Martin?*

Enter MARTIN *combing a Perrywig, and singing.*

GIBBET. The Roads are consumed deep; I'm as dirty as old
Brentford at *Christmas.*—A good pretty Fellow that; who's   105
Servant are you, Friend?

ARCHER. My Master's.

GIBBET. Really?

ARCHER. Really.

GIBBET. That's much.—The Fellow has been at the Bar by his   110
Evasions:—But, pray, Sir, what is your Master's Name?

ARCHER. *Tall, all dall*; [*sings and combs the Perrywig.*] This
is the most obstinate Curl—

GIBBET. I ask you his Name?

ARCHER. Name, Sir,—*Tall, all dall*—I never ask'd him his Name   115
in my Life. *Tall, all dall.*

BONNIFACE. What think you now?

GIBBET. Plain, plain, he talks now as if he were before a Judge:
But, pray, Friend, which way does your Master travel?

ARCHER. A Horseback.   120

GIBBET. Very well again, an old Offender, right;—But, I mean
does he go upwards or downwards?

ARCHER. Downwards, I fear, Sir; *Tall, all.*

GIBBET. I'm afraid my Fate will be a contrary way.

BONNIFACE. Ha, ha, ha! Mr *Martin* you're very arch.—This   125
Gentleman is only travelling towards *Chester*, and wou'd be glad
of your Company, that's all.—Come, Captain, you'll stay to
Night, I suppose; I'll shew you a Chamber—Come, Captain.

GIBBET. Farewel, Friend—

Exit.

ARCHER. Captain, your Servant.—Captain! a pretty Fellow;   130
s'death, I wonder that the Officers of the Army don't conspire
to beat all Scoundrels in Red, but their own.

Enter CHERRY.

CHERRY. [*Aside.*] Gone! and *Martin* here! I hope he did not
listen; I wou'd have the Merit of the discovery all my own,
because I wou'd oblige him to love me. Mr *Martin*, who was that   135
Man with my Father!

ARCHER. Some Recruiting Serjeant, or whip'd out Trooper, I
suppose.

CHERRY. All's safe, I find.

ARCHER. Come, my Dear, have you con'd over the Catechise I   140
taught you last Night?

CHERRY. Come, question me.

ARCHER. What is Love?

CHERRY. Love is I know not what, it comes I know not how,
and goes I know not when.   145

II. II. 129 S.D. *Exit.*] This stage direction should include Bonniface.

ARCHER. Very well, an apt Scholar. [*Chucks her under the Chin.*] Where does Love enter?

CHERRY. Into the Eyes.

ARCHER. And where go out?

CHERRY. I won't tell'ye.   150

ARCHER. What are the Objects of that Passion?

CHERRY. Youth, Beauty, and clean Linen.

ARCHER. The Reason?

CHERRY. The two first are fashionable in Nature, and the third at Court.   155

ARCHER. That's my Dear: What are the Signs and Tokens of that Passion?

CHERRY. A stealing Look, a stammering Tongue, Words improbable, Designs impossible, and Actions impracticable.

ARCHER. That's my good Child, kiss me.—What must a Lover 160 do to obtain his Mistress.

CHERRY. He must adore the Person that disdains him, he must bribe the Chambermaid that betrays him, and court the Footman that laughs at him;—He must, he must—

ARCHER. Nay, Child, I must whip you if you don't mind your 165 Lesson; he must treat his—

CHERRY. O, ay, he must treat his Enemies with Respect, his Friends with Indifference, and all the World with Contempt; he must suffer much, and fear more; he must desire much, and hope little; in short, he must embrace his Ruine, and throw him- 170 self away.

ARCHER. Had ever Man so hopeful a Pupil as mine? come, my Dear, why is Love call'd a Riddle?

CHERRY. Because being blind, he leads those that see, and tho' a Child, he governs a Man.   175

ARCHER. Mighty well.—And why is Love pictur'd blind?

CHERRY. Because the Painters out of the weakness or privilege of their Art chose to hide those Eyes that they cou'd not draw.

ARCHER. That's my dear little Scholar, kiss me again.—And why shou'd Love, that's a Child, govern a Man?   180

CHERRY. Because that a Child is the end of Love.

ARCHER. And so ends Love's Catechism.—And now, my Dear, we'll go in, and make my Master's Bed.

CHERRY. Hold, hold, Mr *Martin*,—You have taken a great deal

of Pains to instruct me, and what d'ye think I have learn't by it? 185
ARCHER.   What?
CHERRY.   That your Discourse and your Habit are Contradic-
tions, and it wou'd be nonsense in me to believe you a Footman
any longer.
ARCHER.   'Oons, what a Witch it is! 190
CHERRY.   Depend upon this, Sir, nothing in this Garb shall ever
tempt me; for tho' I was born to Servitude, I hate it:—Own
your Condition, swear you love me, and then—
ARCHER.   And then we shall go make the Bed.
CHERRY.   Yes. 195
ARCHER.   You must know them, that I am born a Gentleman, my
Education was liberal; but I went to *London* a younger Brother,
fell into the Hands of Sharpers, who stript me of my Money, my
Friends disown'd me, and now my Necessity brings me to what
you see. 200
CHERRY.   Then take my Hands—promise to marry me before you
sleep, and I'll make you Master of two thousand Pound.
ARCHER.   How!
CHERRY.   Two thousand Pound that I have this Minute in my
own Custody; so throw off your Livery this Instant, and I'll go 205
find a Parson.
ARCHER.   What said you? A Parson!
CHERRY.   What! do you scruple?
ARCHER.   Scruple! no, no, but—two thousand Pound you say?
CHERRY.   And better. 210
ARCHER.   S'death, what shall I do—but heark'e, Child, what
need you make me Master of your self and Money, when you
may have the same Pleasure out of me, and still keep your
Fortune in your Hands.
CHERRY.   Then you won't marry me? 215
ARCHER.   I wou'd marry you, but—
CHERRY.   O sweet, Sir, I'm your humble Servant, you're fairly
caught, wou'd you perswade me that any Gentleman who
cou'd bear the Scandal of wearing a Livery, wou'd refuse two
thousand Pound let the Condition be what it wou'd—no, no, 220
Sir,—but I hope you'll Pardon the Freedom I have taken, since it
was only to inform my self of the Respect that I ought to pay you.
                                        Going.

ARCHER. Fairly bit, by *Jupiter*—hold, hold, and have you
    actually two thousand Pound.   225
CHERRY. Sir, I have my Secrets as well as you—when you
    please to be more open, I shall be more free, and be assur'd that
    I have Discoveries that will match yours, be what they will—in
    the mean while be satisfy'd that no Discovery I make shall ever
    hurt you, but beware of my Father.—   230
ARCHER. So—we're like to have as many Adventures in our Inn,
    as *Don Quixote* had in his—let me see,—two thousand Pound!
    if the Wench wou'd promise to dye when the Money were spent,
    I gad, one wou'd marry her, but the Fortune may go off in a Year
    or two, and the Wife may live—Lord knows how long? then an   235
    Inn-keeper's Daughter; ay that's the Devil—there my Pride
    brings me off.

> For whatsoe'er the Sages charge on Pride
> The Angels fall, and twenty Faults beside,
> On Earth I'm sure, 'mong us of mortal Calling,   240
> Pride saves Man oft, and Woman too from falling.

Exit.

End of the Second Act.

ACT III

⟨SCENE I⟩

SCENE *continues*

⟨*A Gallery in* LADY BOUNTIFUL'S *House*⟩

Enter MRS SULLEN, DORINDA.

MRS SULLEN. Ha, ha, ha, my dear Sister, let me embrace thee,
    now we are Friends indeed! for I shall have a Secret of yours, as
    a Pledge for mine—now you'll be good for something, I shall
    have you conversable in the Subjects of the Sex.
DORINDA. But do you think that I am so weak as to fall in Love   5
    with a Fellow at first sight?

MRS SULLEN. Pshaw! now you spoil all, why shou'd not we be
as free in our Friendships as the Men? I warrant you the Gentleman has got to his Confident already, has avow'd his Passion,
toasted your Health, call'd you ten thousand Angels, has run   10
over your Lips, Eyes, Neck, Shape, Air and every thing, in a
Description that warms their Mirth to a second Enjoyment.

DORINDA. Your Hand, Sister, I an't well.

MRS SULLEN. So,—she's breeding already—come Child up
with it—hem a little—so—now tell me, don't you like the   15
Gentleman that we saw at Church just now?

DORINDA. The Man's well enough.

MRS SULLEN. Well enough! is he not a Demigod, a *Narcissus*,
a Star, the Man i'the Moon?

DORINDA. O Sister, I'm extreamly ill.   20

MRS SULLEN. Shall I send to your Mother, Child, for a little of
her Cephalick Plaister to put to the Soals of your Feet, or shall
I send to the Gentleman for something for you?—Come, unlace
your Steas, unbosome your self—the Man is perfectly a pretty
Fellow, I saw him when he first came into Church.   25

DORINDA. I saw him too, Sister, and with an Air that shone,
methought like Rays about his Person.

MRS SULLEN. Well said, up with it.

DORINDA. No forward Coquett Behaviour, no Airs to set him
off, no study'd Looks nor artful Posture,—but Nature did it all—   30

MRS SULLEN. Better and better—one Touch more—come.—

DORINDA. But then his Looks—did you observe his Eyes?

MRS SULLEN. Yes, yes, I did—his Eyes, well, what of his Eyes?

DORINDA. Sprightly, but not wandring; they seem'd to view,
but never gaz'd on any thing but me—and then his Looks so   35
humble were, and yet so noble, that they aim'd to tell me that
he cou'd with Pride dye at my Feet, tho' he scorn'd Slavery any
where else.

MRS SULLEN. The Physick works purely—How d'ye find your
self now, my Dear?   40

DORINDA. Hem! much better, my Dear—O here comes our
Mercury! [*Enter* SCRUB.] Well *Scrub*, what News of the Gentleman?

SCRUB. Madam, I have brought you a Packet of News.

DORINDA. Open it quickly, come.   45

SCRUB. In the first place I enquir'd who the Gentleman was? they told me he was a Stranger. Secondly, I ask'd what the Gentleman was, they answer'd and said, that they never saw him before. Thirdly, I enquir'd what Countryman he was, they reply'd 'twas more than they knew. Fourthly, I demanded 50 whence he came, their Answer was, they cou'd not tell. And Fifthly, I ask'd whither he went, and they reply'd they knew nothing of the matter,—and this is all I cou'd learn.

MRS SULLEN. But what do the People say, can't they guess?

SCRUB. Why some think he's a Spy, some guess he's a Mounte- 55 bank, some say one thing, some another; but for my own part, I believe he's a Jesuit,

DORINDA. A Jesuit! why a Jesuit?

SCRUB. Because he keeps his Horses always ready sadled, and his Footman talks French. 60

MRS SULLEN. His Footman!

SCRUB. Ay, he and the Count's Footman were Gabbering French like two intreaguing Ducks in a Mill-Pond, and I believe they talk'd of me, for they laugh'd consumedly.

DORINDA. What sort of Livery has the Footman? 65

SCRUB. Livery! Lord, Madam, I took him for a Captain, he's so bedizen'd with Lace, and then he has Tops to his Shoes, up to his mid Leg, a silver headed Cane dangling at his Nuckles,—he carries his Hands in his Pockets just so—[*Walks in the French Air*] and has a fine long Perriwig ty'd up in a Bag—Lord, 70 Madam, he's clear another sort of Man than I.

MRS SULLEN. That may easily be—but what shall we do now, Sister?

DORINDA. I have it—This Fellow has a world of Simplicity, and some Cunning, the first hides the latter by abundance— 75 *Scrub.*

SCRUB. Madam.

DORINDA. We have a great mind to know who this Gentleman is, only for our Satisfaction.

SCRUB. Yes, Madam, it would be a Satisfaction, no doubt. 80

DORINDA. You must go and get acquainted with his Footman, and invite him hither to drink a Bottle of your Ale, because you're Butler to Day.

SCRUB. Yes, Madam, I am Butler every Sunday.

MRS SULLEN. O brave, Sister, O my Conscience, you under-   85
stand the Mathematicks already—'tis the best Plot in the World;
your Mother, you know, will be gone to Church, my Spouse will
be got to the Ale-house with his Scoundrels, and the House will
be our own—so we drop in by Accident and ask the Fellow
some Questions our selves. In the Countrey you know any   90
Stranger is Company, and we're glad to take up with the
Butler in a Country Dance, and happy if he'll do us the Favour.

SCRUB. Oh! Madam, you wrong me, I never refus'd your Ladyship the Favour in my Life.

Enter GIPSEY.

GIPSEY. Ladies, Dinner's upon Table.   95

DORINDA. *Scrub*, We'll excuse your waiting—Go where we
order'd you.

SCRUB. I shall.

Exeunt.

⟨SCENE II⟩

SCENE, *changes to the Inn.*

Enter AIMWELL *and* ARCHER.

ARCHER. Well, *Tom*, I find you're a Marksman.

AIMWELL. A Marksman! who so blind cou'd be, as not discern
a Swan among the Ravens.

ARCHER. Well, but heark'ee, *Aimwell.*

AIMWELL. *Aimwell*! call me *Oroondates, Cesario, Amadis*, all   5
that Romance can in a Lover paint, and then I'll answer. O
Archer, I read her thousands in her Looks, she look'd like *Ceres*
in her Harvest, Corn, Wine and Oil, Milk and Honey, Gardens,
Groves and Purling Streams play'd on her plenteous Face.

ARCHER. Her Face! her Pocket, you mean; the Corn, Wine and   10
Oil lies there. In short, she has ten thousand Pound, that's the
English on't.

AIMWELL. Her Eyes—

ARCHER. Are Demi-Cannons to be sure, so I won't stand their
Battery.   15

Going.

AIMWELL. Pray excuse me, my Passion must have vent.
ARCHER. Passion! what a plague, d'ee think these Romantick
  Airs will do our Business? Were my Temper as extravagant as
  yours, my Adventures have something more Romantick by half.
AIMWELL. Your Adventures!   20
ARCHER. Yes,

> The Nymph that with her twice ten hundred Pounds
> With brazen Engine hot, and Quoif clear starch'd
> Can fire the Guest in warming of the Bed—

There's a Touch of Sublime *Milton* for you, and the Subject   25
but an Inn-keeper's Daughter; I can play with a Girl as an
Angler do's with his Fish; he keeps it at the end of his Line,
runs it up the Stream, and down the Stream, till at last, he brings
it to hand, tickles the Trout, and so whips it into his Basket.

Enter BONNIFACE.

BONNIFACE. Mr *Martin*, as the saying is—yonder's an honest   30
  Fellow below, my Lady *Bountiful's* Butler, who begs the
  Honour that you wou'd go Home with him and see his Cellar.
ARCHER. Do my *Baisemains* to the Gentleman, and tell him I
  will do my self the Honour to wait on him immediately.

                                        Exit BONNIFACE.

AIMWELL. What do I hear? soft *Orpheus* Play, and fair *Toftida*   35
  sing?
ARCHER. Pshaw! damn your Raptures, I tell you here's a Pump
  going to be put into the Vessel, and the Ship will get into
  Harbour, my Life on't. You say there's another Lady very hand-
  some there.   40
AIMWELL. Yes, faith.
ARCHER. I'm in love with her already.
AIMWELL. Can't you give me a Bill upon *Cherry* in the mean time.
ARCHER. No, no, Friend, all her Corn, Wine and Oil is in-
  gross'd to my Market.—And once more I warn you to keep your   45
  Anchorage clear of mine, for if you fall foul of me, by this Light
  you shall go to the Bottom.—What! make Prize of my little
  Frigat, while I am upon the Cruise for you.

                                        Exit.

Enter BONNIFACE.

AIMWELL. Well, well, I won't—Landlord, have you any tolerable Company in the House, I don't care for dining alone.   50

BONNIFACE. Yes, Sir, there's a Captain below; as the saying is,
that arrived about an Hour ago.

AIMWELL. Gentlemen of his Coat are welcome every where;
will you make him a Complement from me, and tell him I should
be glad of his Company.   55

BONNIFACE. Who shall I tell him, Sir, wou'd.—

AIMWELL. Ha! that Stroak was well thrown in—I'm only a
Traveller like himself, and wou'd be glad of his Company, that's
all.

BONNIFACE. I obey your Commands, as the saying is.   60

Exit.

Enter ARCHER.

ARCHER. S'Death! I had forgot, what Title will you give your
self?

AIMWELL. My Brother's to be sure, he wou'd never give me any
thing else, so I'll make bold with his Honour this bout—you
know the rest of your Cue.   65

ARCHER. Ay, ay.

Exit ARCHER.

Enter GIBBET.

GIBBET. Sir, I'm yours.

AIMWELL. 'Tis more than I deserve, Sir, for I don't know you.

GIBBET. I don't wonder at that, Sir, for you never saw me
before, (*Aside.*) I hope.   70

AIMWELL. And pray, Sir, how came I by the Honour of seeing
you now?

GIBBET. Sir, I scorn to intrude upon any Gentleman—but my
Landlord—

AIMWELL. O, Sir, I ask your Pardon, you're the Captain he told   75
me of.

GIBBET. At your Service, Sir.

AIMWELL. What Regiment, may I be so bold?

III. II. 65 S.D. *Exit* ARCHER] *Exit.* Bon. 1707, C, W; *Exit.* 1707².

GIBBET.　A marching Regiment, Sir, an old Corps.

AIMWELL.　[*Aside.*] Very old, if your Coat be Regimental. 80
You have serv'd abroad, Sir?

GIBBET.　Yes, Sir, in the Plantations, 'twas my Lot to be sent into
the worst Service, I wou'd have quitted it indeed, but a Man of
Honour, you know—Besides 'twas for the good of my Country
that I shou'd be abroad—Any thing for the good of one's 85
Country—I'm a *Roman* for that.

AIMWELL.　[*Aside.*] One of the first, I'll lay my Life.
You found the *West Indies* very hot, Sir?

GIBBET.　Aӱ, Sir, too hot for me.

AIMWELL.　Pray, Sir, han't I seen your Face at *Will's* Coffee- 90
house?

GIBBET.　Yes, Sir, and at *White's* too.

AIMWELL.　And where is your Company now, Captain?

GIBBET.　They an't come yet.

AIMWELL.　Why, d'ye expect 'em here? 95

GIBBET.　They'll be here to Night, Sir.

AIMWELL.　Which way do they march?

GIBBET.　Across the Country—⟨*Aside.*⟩ the Devil's in't, if I han't
said enough to encourage him to declare—but I'm afraid he's not
right, I must tack about. 100

AIMWELL.　Is your Company to quarter in *Litchfield*?

GIBBET.　In this House, Sir.

AIMWELL.　What! all?

GIBBET.　My Company's but thin, ha, ha, ha, we are but three,
ha, ha, ha. 105

AIMWELL.　You're merry, Sir.

GIBBET.　Ay, Sir, you must excuse me, Sir, I understand the
World, especially, the Art of Travelling; I don't care, Sir, for
answering Questions directly upon the Road—for I generally
ride with a Charge about me. 110

AIMWELL.　[*Aside.*] Three or four, I believe.

GIBBET.　I am credibly inform'd that there are Highway-men upon
this Quarter, not, Sir, that I cou'd suspect a Gentleman of your
Figure—But truly, Sir, I have got such a way of Evasion upon
the Road, that I don't care for speaking Truth to any Man. 115

AIMWELL.　Your Caution may be necessary—Then I presume
you're no Captain?

GIBBET. Not I, Sir, Captain is a good travelling Name, and so
I take it; it stops a great many foolish Inquiries that are generally
made about Gentlemen that travel, it gives a Man on Air of some-   120
thing, and makes the Drawers obedient—And thus far I am a
Captain, and no farther.

AIMWELL. And pray, Sir, what is your true Profession?

GIBBET. O, Sir, you must excuse me—upon my Word, Sir, I
don't think it safe to tell you.   125

AIMWELL. Ha, ha, ha, upon my word I commend you.

Enter BONNIFACE.

Well, Mr. *Bonniface*, what's the News?

BONNIFACE. There's another Gentleman below, as the saying
is, that hearing you were but two, wou'd be glad to make the
third Man if you wou'd give him leave.   130

AIMWELL. What is he?

BONNIFACE. A Clergyman, as the saying is.

AIMWELL. A Clergyman! is he really a Clergyman? or is it only
his travelling Name, as my Friend the Captain has it.

BONNIFACE. O, Sir, he's a Priest and Chaplain to the French   135
Officers in Town.

AIMWELL. Is he a French-man?

BONNIFACE. Yes, Sir, born at *Brussels*.

GIBBET. A French-man, and a Priest! I won't be seen in his
Company, Sir; I have a Value for my Reputation, Sir.   140

AIMWELL. Nay, but Captain, since we are by our selves—Can he
speak English, Landlord?

BONNIFACE. Very well, Sir, you may know him, as the saying
is, to be a Foreigner by his Accent, and that's all.

AIMWELL. Then he has been in *England* before?   145

BONNIFACE. Never, Sir, but he's a Master of Languages, as the
saying is, he talks Latin, it do's me good to hear him talk Latin.

AIMWELL. Then you understand Latin, Mr. *Bonniface*?

BONNIFACE. Not I, Sir, as the saying is, but he talks it so very
fast that I'm sure it must be good.   150

AIMWELL. Pray desire him to walk up.

BONNIFACE. Here he is, as the saying is.

Enter FOIGARD.

FOIGARD. Save you, Gentlemen's, both.

AIMWELL. A French-man! Sir, your most humble Servant.

FOIGARD. Och, dear Joy, I am your most faithful Shervant, and 155
yours alsho.

GIBBET. Doctor, you talk very good English, but you have a
mighty Twang of the Foreigner.

FOIGARD. My English is very vel for the vords, but we Foregners
you know cannot bring our Tongues about the Pronunciation so 160
soon.

AIMWELL. [*Aside.*] A Foreigner! a down-right Teague by this
Light.
Were you born in *France*, Doctor.

FOIGARD. I was educated in *France*, but I was borned at *Brussels*, 165
I am a Subject of the King of *Spain*, Joy.

GIBBET. What King of *Spain*, Sir, speak.

FOIGARD. Upon my Shoul Joy, I cannot tell you as yet.

AIMWELL. Nay, Captain, that was too hard upon the Doctor,
he's a Stranger. 170

FOIGARD. O let him alone, dear Joy, I am of a Nation that is
not easily put out of Countenance.

AIMWELL. Come, Gentlemen, I'll end the Dispute.—Here,
Landlord, is Dinner ready?

BONNIFACE. Upon the Table, as the saying is. 175

AIMWELL. Gentlemen—pray—that Door—

FOIGARD. No, no fait, the Captain must lead.

AIMWELL. No, Doctor, the Church is our Guide.

GIBBET. Ay, ay, so it is.—

Exit foremost, they follow.

⟨SCENE III⟩

SCENE, *Changes to a Gallery in* LADY BOUNTIFUL'*s House.*

Enter ARCHER *and* SCRUB *singing, and hugging one another,* SCRUB
with a Tankard in his Hand, GIPSEY *listning at a distance.*

SCRUB. *Tall, all dall*—Come, my dear Boy—Let's have that
Song once more.

ARCHER. No, no, we shall disturb the Family;—But will you be
sure to keep the Secret?

SCRUB. Pho! upon my Honour, as I'm a Gentleman.   5

ARCHER. 'Tis enough.—You must know then that my Master is
the Lord Viscount *Aimwell*; he fought a Duel t'other day in
London, wounded his Man so dangerously, that he thinks fit to
withdraw till he hears whether the Gentleman's Wounds be
mortal or not: He never was in this part of *England* before, so he   10
chose to retire to this Place, that's all.

GIPSEY. And that's enough for me.

Exit.

SCRUB. And where were you when your Master fought?

ARCHER. We never know of our Masters Quarrels.

SCRUB. No! if our Masters in the Country here receive a Chal-   15
lenge, the first thing they do is to tell their Wives; the Wife tells
the Servants, the Servants alarm the Tenants, and in half an
Hour you shall have the whole County in Arms.

ARCHER. To hinder two Men from doing what they have no
mind for:—But if you should chance to talk now of my Business?   20

SCRUB. Talk! ay, Sir, had I not learn't the knack of holding my
Tongue, I had never liv'd so long in a great Family.

ARCHER. Ay, ay, to be sure there are Secrets in all Families.

SCRUB. Secrets, ay;—But I'll say no more.—Come, sit down,
we'll make an end of our Tankard: Here—   25

ARCHER. With all my Heart; who knows but you and I may
come to be better acquainted, eh—Here's your Ladies Healths;
you have three, I think, and to be sure there must be Secrets
among 'em.

SCRUB. Secrets! Ay, Friend; I wish I had a Friend—   30

ARCHER. Am not I your Friend? come, you and I will be sworn
Brothers.

SCRUB. Shall we?

ARCHER. From this Minute.—Give me a kiss—And now
Brother *Scrub*—   35

SCRUB. And now, Brother *Martin*, I will tell you a Secret that
will make your Hair stand on end:—You must know, that I am
consumedly in Love.

ARCHER. That's a terrible Secret, that's the Truth on't.

SCRUB. That Jade, *Gipsey*, that was with us just now in the   40

Cellar, is the arrantest Whore that ever wore a Petticoat; and I'm dying for love of her.

ARCHER. Ha, ha, ha—Are you in love with her Person, or her Vertue, Brother *Scrub*?

SCRUB. I should like Vertue best, because it is more durable than Beauty; for Vertue holds good with some Women long, and many a Day after they have lost it.

ARCHER. In the Country, I grant ye, where no Woman's Vertue is lost, till a Bastard be found.

SCRUB. Ay, cou'd I bring her to a Bastard, I shou'd have her all to my self; but I dare not put it upon that Lay, for fear of being sent for a Soldier.—Pray, Brother, how do you Gentlemen in *London* like that same Pressing Act?

ARCHER. Very ill, Brother *Scrub*;—'Tis the worst that ever was made for us: Formerly I remember the good Days, when we cou'd dun our Masters for our Wages, and if they refused to pay us, we cou'd have a Warrant to carry 'em before a Justice; but now if we talk of eating, they have a Warrant for us, and carry us before three Justices.

SCRUB. And to be sure we go, if we talk of eating; for the Justices won't give their own Servants a bad Example. Now this is my Misfortune—I dare not speak in the House, while that Jade *Gipsey* dings about like a Fury—Once I had the better end of the Staff.

ARCHER. And how comes the Change now?

SCRUB. Why, the Mother of all this Mischief is a Priest.

ARCHER. A Priest!

SCRUB. Ay, a damn'd Son of a Whore of *Babylon*, that came over hither to say Grace to the *French* Officers, and eat up our Provisions—There's not a Day goes over his Head without Dinner or Supper in this House.

ARCHER. How came he so familiar in the Family?

SCRUB. Because he speaks *English* as if he had liv'd here all his Life; and tells Lies as if he had been a Traveller from his Cradle.

ARCHER. And this Priest, I'm afraid has converted the Affections of your *Gipsey*.

SCRUB. Converted! ay, and perverted, my dear Friend:—For I'm afraid he has made her a Whore and a Papist.—But this is not

C

all; there's the *French* Count and Mrs *Sullen*, they're in the Con-
federacy, and for some private Ends of their own to be sure.   80

ARCHER. A very hopeful Family yours, Brother *Scrub*; I suppose
the Maiden Lady has her Lover too.

SCRUB. Not that I know;—She's the best on 'em, that's the Truth
on't: But they take care to prevent my Curiosity, by giving me
so much Business, that I'm a perfect Slave.—What d'ye think is   85
my Place in this Family?

ARCHER. Butler, I suppose.

SCRUB. Ah, Lord help you—I'll tell you—Of a *Monday*, I drive
the Coach; of a *Tuesday*, I drive the Plough; on *Wednesday*, I
follow the Hounds; a *Thursday*, I dun the Tenants; on *Fryday*,   90
I go to Market; on *Saturday*, I draw Warrants; and a *Sunday*, I
draw Beer.

ARCHER. Ha, ha, ha! if variety be a Pleasure in Life, you have
enough on't, my dear Brother—But what Ladies are those?

SCRUB. Ours, ours; that upon the right Hand is Mrs. *Sullen*, and   95
the other is Mrs *Dorinda*.—Don't mind 'em, sit still, Man—

Enter MRS SULLEN, *and* DORINDA.

MRS SULLEN. I have heard my Brother talk of my Lord *Aimwell*,
but they say that his Brother is the finer Gentleman.

DORINDA. That's impossible, Sister.

MRS SULLEN. He's vastly rich, but very close, they say.   100

DORINDA. No matter for that; if I can creep into his Heart, I'll
open his Breast, I warrant him: I have heard say, that People may
be guess'd at by the Behaviour of their Servants; I cou'd wish we
might talk to that Fellow.

MRS SULLEN. So do I; for, I think he's a very pretty Fellow: 105
Come this way, I'll throw out a Lure for him presently.

> *They walk a turn towards the opposite side of the Stage,*
> MRS SULLEN *drops her Glove,* ARCHER *runs, takes*
> *it up, and gives it to her.*

ARCHER. Corn, Wine, and Oil, indeed—But, I think, the Wife
has the greatest plenty of Flesh and Blood; she should be my
Choice—Ah, a, say you so—Madam—Your Ladyship's Glove.

III. III. 95. SCRUB. Ours, ours] s (who gives c [1707] as his authority); *Arch.*
Ours, ours, 1707, 1707², c, w.

MRS SULLEN. O, Sir, I thank you—what a handsom Bow the 110
Fellow has?

DORINDA. Bow! why I have known several Footman come down
from *London* set up here for Dancing-Masters, and carry off the
best Fortunes in the Country.

ARCHER. [*Aside.*] That Project, for ought I know, had been 115
better than ours, Brother *Scrub*—Why don't you introduce me.

SCRUB. Ladies, this is the strange Gentleman's Servant that you
see at Church to Day; I understood he came from *London*, and
so I invited him to the Cellar, that he might show me the newest
Flourish in whetting my Knives. 120

DORINDA. And I hope you have made much of him?

ARCHER. O yes, Madam, but the Strength of your Ladyship's
Liquor is a little too potent for the Constitution of your humble
Servant.

MRS SULLEN. What, then you don't usually drink Ale? 125

ARCHER. No, Madam, my constant Drink is Tea, or a little Wine
and Water; 'tis prescrib'd me by the Physician for a Remedy
against the Spleen.

SCRUB. O la, O la!—a Footman have the Spleen.—

MRS SULLEN. I thought that Distemper had been only proper 130
to People of Quality.

ARCHER. Madam, like all other Fashions it wears out, and so
descends to their Servants; tho' in a great many of us, I believe
it proceeds from some melancholly Particles in the Blood,
occasion'd by the Stagnation of Wages. 135

DORINDA. How affectedly the Fellow talks—How long, pray,
have you serv'd your present Master?

ARCHER. Not long; my Life has been mostly spent in the Service
of the Ladies.

MRS SULLEN. And pray, which Service do you like best? 140

ARCHER. Madam, the Ladies pay best; the Honour of serving
them is sufficient Wages; there is a Charm in their looks that
delivers a Pleasure with their Commands, and gives our Duty
the Wings of Inclination.

MRS SULLEN. ⟨*To* DORINDA.⟩ That Flight was above the 145
pitch of a Livery; ⟨*To* ARCHER⟩ and, Sir, wou'd not you be
satisfied to serve a Lady again?

ARCHER. As a Groom of the Chamber, Madam, but not as a Footman.

MRS SULLEN. I suppose you serv'd as Footman before.   15c

ARCHER. For that Reason I wou'd not serve in that Post again; for my Memory is too weak for the load of Messages that the Ladies lay upon their Servants in *London*; my Lady *Howd'ye*, the last Mistress I serv'd call'd me up one Morning, and told me, *Martin*, go to my Lady *Allnight* with my humble Service; tell   155 her I was to wait on her Ladyship yesterday, and left word with Mrs. *Rebecca*, that the Preliminaries of the Affair she knows of, are stopt till we know the concurrence of the Person that I know of, for which there are Circumstances wanting which we shall accommodate at the old Place; but that in the mean time there is   16c a Person about her Ladyship, that from several Hints and Surmises, was accessary at a certain time to the disappointments that naturally attend things, that to her knowledge are of more Importance.

MRS SULLEN. } Ha, ha, ha! where are you going, Sir?   16
DORINDA.

ARCHER. Why, I han't half done.—The whole Howd'ye was about half an Hour long; so I hapned to misplace two Syllables, and was turn'd off, and render'd incapable—

DORINDA. The pleasantest Fellow, Sister, I ever saw.—But, Friend, if your Master be marry'd,—I presume you still serve a   17c Lady.

ARCHER. No, Madam, I take care never to come into a marry'd Family; the Commands of the Master and Mistress are always so contrary, that 'tis impossible to please both.

DORINDA. [*Aside.*] There's a main point gain'd.—My Lord is   17 not marry'd, I find.

MRS SULLEN. But, I wonder, Friend, that in so many good Services, you had not a better Provision made for you.

ARCHER. I don't know how, Madam.—I had a Lieutenancy offer'd me three or four Times; but that is not Bread, Madam—   18c I live much better as I do.

SCRUB. Madam, he sings rarely.—I was thought to do pretty well here in the Country till he came; but alack a day, I'm nothing to my Brother *Martin*.

DORINDA. Does he? Pray, Sir, will you oblige us with a Song?   18

ARCHER. Are you for Passion, or Humour?

SCRUB. O le! he has the purest Ballad about a Trifle—

MRS SULLEN. A Trifle! pray, Sir, let's have it.

ARCHER. I'm asham'd to offer you a Trifle, Madam: But since
　　you command me—　　　　　　　　　　　　　　　　　　190

Sings to the Tune of Sir Simon *the King.*

A Trifling Song you shall hear,
Begun with a Trifle and ended:
All Trifling People draw near,
And I shall be nobly attended.

Were it not for Trifles, a few,　　　　　　195
That lately have come into Play;
The Men wou'd want something to do,
And the Women want something to say.

What makes Men trifle in Dressing?
Because the Ladies (they know)　　　　　200
Admire, by often Possessing,
That eminent Trifle a Beau.

When the Lover his Moments has trifled,
The Trifle of Trifles to gain:
No sooner the Virgin is Rifled,　　　　　205
But a Trifle shall part 'em again.

What mortal Man wou'd be able
At *White's* half an Hour to sit?
Or who cou'd bear a Tea-Table,
Without talking of Trifles for Wit?　　　　210

The Court is from Trifles secure,
Gold Keys are no Trifles, we see:
White Rods are no Trifles, I'm sure,
Whatever their Bearers may be.

191–242. A Trifling Song . . .] The first two lines of the song are printed in
707, 1707², c, w; the full text is taken from *The Dramatick Works* (1736) where
t is printed after the Epilogue.

But if you will go to the Place,   215
Where Trifles abundantly breed,
The Levee will show you his Grace
Makes Promises Trifles indeed.

A Coach with six Footmen behind,
I count neither Trifle nor Sin: 220
But, ye Gods! how oft do we find
A scandalous Trifle within?

A flask of Champaign, People think it
A Trifle, or something as bad:
But if you'll contrive how to drink it,   225
You'll find it no Trifle egad.

A Parson's a Trifle at Sea,
A Widow's a Trifle in Sorrow:
A Peace is a Trifle to-day,
Who knows what may happen to-morrow?   230

A Black Coat, a Trifle may cloak,
Or to hide it, the Red may endeavour:
But if once the Army is broke,
We shall have more Trifles than ever.

The Stage is a Trifle, they say,   235
The Reason, pray carry along,
Because at ev'ry new Play,
The House they with Trifles so throng.

But with People's Malice to Trifle,
And to set us all on a Foot: 240
The Author of this is a Trifle,
And his Song is a Trifle to boot.

MRS SULLEN.   Very well, Sir, we're obliged to you.—Something for a pair of Gloves.

Offering him Money.

ARCHER. I humbly beg leave to be excused: My Master, Madam, 245
  pays me; nor dare I take Money from any other Hand without
  injuring his Honour, and disobeying his Commands.

Exit.

DORINDA. This is surprising: Did you ever see so pretty a well
  bred Fellow?
MRS SULLEN. The Devil take him for wearing that Livery.   250
DORINDA. I fancy, Sister, he may be some Gentleman, a Friend
  of my Lords, that his Lordship has pitch'd upon for his Courage,
  Fidelity, and Discretion to bear him Company in this Dress, and
  who, ten to one was his Second too.
MRS SULLEN. It is so, it must be so, and it shall be so:—For I 255
  like him.
DORINDA. What! better than the Count?
MRS SULLEN. The Count happen'd to be the most agreeable
  Man upon the Place; and so I chose him to serve me in my
  Design upon my Husband.—But I shou'd like this Fellow better 260
  in a Design upon my self.
DORINDA. But now, Sister, for an Interview with this Lord, and
  this Gentleman; how shall we bring that about?
MRS SULLEN. Patience! you Country Ladies give no Quarter,
  if once you be enter'd.—Wou'd you prevent their Desires, and 265
  give the Fellows no wishing-time.—Look'ye, *Dorinda*, if my
  Lord *Aimwell* loves you or deserves you, he'll find a way to see
  you, and there we must leave it.—My Business comes now upon
  the Tapis—Have you prepar'd your Brother?
DORINDA. Yes, yes.   270
MRS SULLEN. And how did he relish it?
DORINDA. He said little, mumbled something to himself,
  promis'd to be guided by me: But here he comes—

Enter SULLEN.

SULLEN. What singing was that I heard just now?
MRS SULLEN. The singing in your Head, my Dear, you   275
  complain'd of it all Day.
SULLEN. You're impertinent.
MRS SULLEN. I was ever so, since I became one Flesh with you.
SULLEN. One Flesh! rather two Carcasses join'd unnaturally
  together.   280

MRS SULLEN. Or rather a living Soul coupled to a dead Body.

DORINDA. So, this is fine Encouragement for me.

SULLEN. Yes, my Wife shews you what you must do.

MRS SULLEN. And my Husband shews you what you must suffer.

SULLEN. S'death, why can't you be silent?   285

MRS SULLEN. S'death, why can't you talk?

SULLEN. Do you talk to any purpose?

MRS SULLEN. Do you think to any purpose?

SULLEN. Sister, heark'ye; (*Whispers.*) I shan't be home till it be
late.   290

> *Exit.*

MRS SULLEN. What did he whisper to ye?

DORINDA. That he wou'd go round the back way, come into the
Closet, and listen as I directed him.—But let me beg you once
more, dear Sister, to drop this Project; for, as I told you before,
instead of awaking him to Kindness, you may provoke him to a   295
Rage; and then who knows how far his Brutality may carry him?

MRS SULLEN. I'm provided to receive him, I warrant you: But
here comes the Count, vanish.

> *Exit* DORINDA.

Enter COUNT BELLAIR.

Don't you wonder, *Monsieur le Count*, that I was not at Church
this Afternoon?   300

COUNT. I more wonder, Madam, that you go dere at all, or how
you dare to lift those Eyes to Heaven that are guilty of so much
killing.

MRS SULLEN. If Heaven, Sir, has given to my Eyes with the
Power of killing, the Virtue of making a Cure, I hope the one   305
may atone for the other.

COUNT. O largely, Madam; wou'd your Ladyship be as ready to
apply the Remedy as to give the Wound?—Consider, Madam,
I am doubly a Prisoner; first to the Arms of your General, then
to your more conquering Eyes; my first Chains are easy, there a   310
Ransom may redeem me, but from your Fetters I never shall get
free.

MRS SULLEN. Alas, Sir, why shou'd you complain to me of
your Captivity, who am in Chains my self? you know, Sir, that

I am bound, nay, must be tied up in that particular that might 315
give you ease: I am like you, a Prisoner of War—Of War indeed:
—I have given my Parole of Honour; wou'd you break yours to
gain your Liberty?

COUNT.   Most certainly I wou'd, were I a Prisoner among the
Turks; dis is your Case; you're a Slave, Madam, Slave to the 320
worst of *Turks*, a Husband.

MRS SULLEN.   There lies my Foible, I confess; no Fortifications,
no Courage, Conduct, nor Vigilancy can pretend to defend a
Place, where the Cruelty of the Governour forces the Garrison
to Mutiny.   325

COUNT.   And where de Besieger is resolv'd to die before de Place
—Here will I fix; [*Kneels.*] With Tears, Vows, and Prayers
assault your Heart, and never rise till you surrender; or if I
must storm—Love and St. *Michael*—And so I begin the
Attack—   330

MRS SULLEN.   Stand off—[*Aside.*] Sure he hears me not—And I
cou'd almost wish he—did not.—The Fellow makes love very
prettily. But, Sir, why shou'd you put such a Value upon my
Person, when you see it despis'd by one that knows it so much
better.   335

COUNT.   He knows it not, tho' he possesses it; if he but knew the
Value of the Jewel he is Master of, he wou'd always wear it next
his Heart, and sleep with it in his Arms.

MRS SULLEN.   But since he throws me unregarded from him.

COUNT.   And one that knows your Value well, comes by, and 340
takes you up, is it not Justice.

                                        Goes to lay hold on her.

Enter SULLEN *with his Sword drawn.*

SULLEN.   Hold, Villain, hold.

MRS SULLEN.   [*Presenting a Pistol.*] Do you hold.

SULLEN.   What! Murther your Husband, to defend your Bully.

MRS SULLEN.   Bully! for shame, Mr. *Sullen*; Bullies wear long 345
Swords, the Gentleman has none, he's a Prisoner you know—I
was aware of your Outrage, and prepar'd this to receive your
Violence, and, if Occasion were, to preserve my self against the
Force of this other Gentleman.

                315. must be] 1707², c, w; most be 1707.

COUNT. O Madam, your Eyes be bettre Fire Arms than your   350
Pistol, they nevre miss.

SULLEN. What! court my Wife to my Face!

MRS SULLEN. Pray, Mr. *Sullen*, put up, suspend your Fury for a
Minute.

SULLEN. To give you time to invent an Excuse.   355

MRS SULLEN. I need none.

SULLEN. No, for I heard every Sillable of your Discourse.

COUNT. Ay! and begar, I tink de Dialogue was vera pretty.

MRS SULLEN. Then I suppose, Sir, you heard something of
your own Barbarity.   360

SULLEN. Barbarity! Oons what does the Woman call Barbarity?
do I ever meddle with you?

MRS SULLEN. No.

SULLEN. As for you, Sir, I shall take another time.

COUNT. Ah, begar, and so must I.   365

SULLEN. Look'e, Madam, don't think that my Anger proceeds
from any Concern I have for your Honour, but for my own, and
if you can contrive any way of being a Whore without making
me a Cuckold, do it and welcome.

MRS SULLEN. Sir, I thank you kindly, you wou'd allow me the   370
Sin but rob me of the Pleasure—No, no, I'm resolv'd never to
venture upon the Crime without the Satisfaction of seeing you
punish'd for't.

SULLEN. Then will you grant me this, my Dear? let any Body
else do you the Favour but that French-man, for I mortally hate   375
his whole Generation.

Exit.

COUNT. Ah, Sir, that be ungrateful, for begar, I love some of
your's, Madam.—

Approaching her.

MRS SULLEN. No, Sir.—

COUNT. No, Sir,—Garzoon, Madam, I am not your Husband.   380

MRS SULLEN. 'Tis time to undeceive you, Sir,—I believ'd your
Addresses to me were no more than an Amusement, and I hope
you will think the same of my Complaisance, and to convince
you that you ought, you must know, that I brought you hither
only to make you instrumental in setting me right with my   385
Husband, for he was planted to listen by my Appointment.

COUNT. By your Appointment?

MRS SULLEN. Certainly.

COUNT. And so, Madam, while I was telling twenty Stories to part you from your Husband, begar, I was bringing you together all the while. 390

MRS SULLEN. I ask your Pardon, Sir, but I hope this will give you a Taste of the Vertue of the English Ladies.

COUNT. Begar, Madam, your Vertue be vera Great, but Garzoon your Honeste be vera little. 395

Enter DORINDA.

MRS SULLEN. Nay, now you're angry, Sir.

COUNT. Angry! fair *Dorinda*.

Sings Dorinda *the Opera Tune*
and addresses to DORINDA,

Madam, when your Ladyship want a Fool, send for me, fair *Dorinda, Revenge, etc.*

Exit.

MRS SULLEN. There goes the true Humour of his Nation, Resentment with good Manners, and the height of Anger in a Song,—Well Sister, you must be Judge, for you have heard the Trial. 400

DORINDA. And I bring in my Brother Guilty.

MRS SULLEN. But I must bear the Punishment,—'Tis hard Sister. 405

DORINDA. I own it—but you must have Patience.

MRS SULLEN. Patience! the Cant of Custom—Providence sends no Evil without a Remedy—shou'd I lie groaning under a Yoke I can shake off, I were accessary to my Ruin, and my Patience were no better than self-Murder. 410

DORINDA. But how can you shake off the Yoke—Your Divisions don't come within the Reach of the Law for a Divorce.

MRS SULLEN. Law! what Law can search into the remote Abyss of Nature, what Evidence can prove the unaccountable Disaffections of Wedlock—can a Jury sum up the endless Aversions that are rooted in our Souls, or can a Bench give Judgment upon Antipathies. 415

DORINDA. They never pretend it Sister, they never meddle but in case of Uncleanness. 420

MRS SULLEN.   Uncleanness! O Sister, casual Violation is a
transient Injury, and may possibly be repair'd, but can radical
Hatreds be ever reconcil'd—No, no, Sister, Nature is the first
Lawgiver, and when she has set Tempers opposite, not all the
golden Links of Wedlock, nor Iron Manacles of Law can keep   425
'um fast.

> *Wedlock we own ordain'd by Heaven's Decree,*
> *But such as Heaven ordain'd it first to be,*
> *Concurring Tempers in the Man and Wife*
> *As mutual Helps to draw the Load of Life.*   430
> *View all the Works of Providence above,*
> *The Stars with Harmony and Concord move;*
> *View all the Works of Providence below,*
> *The Fire, the Water, Earth, and Air, we know*
> *All in one Plant agree to make it grow.*   435
> *Must Man the chiefest Work of Art Divine,*
> *Be doom'd in endless Discord to repine.*
> *No, we shou'd injure Heaven by that surmise*
> *Omnipotence is just, were Man but wise.*

End of the Third Act.

ACT IV

⟨SCENE I⟩

SCENE, *continues.*

Enter MRS SULLEN.

MRS SULLEN.   Were I born an humble Turk, where Women have
no Soul nor Property there I must sit contented—But in
England, a Country whose Women are it's Glory, must Women
be abus'd, where Women rule, must Women be enslav'd? nay,
cheated into Slavery, mock'd by a Promise of comfortable   5

Society into a Wilderness of Solitude—I dare not keep the
Thought about me—O, here comes something to divert me—

Enter a COUNTRY WOMAN.

WOMAN. I come an't please your Ladyship, you're my Lady
Bountiful, an't ye?

MRS SULLEN. Well, good Woman go on.   10

WOMAN. I come seventeen long Mail to have a Cure for my
Husband's sore Leg.

MRS SULLEN. Your Husband! what Woman, cure your Husband!

WOMAN. Ay, poor Man, for his sore Leg won't let him stir from   15
Home.

MRS SULLEN. There, I confess, you have given me a Reason.
Well good Woman, I'll tell you what you must do—You must
lay your Husband's Leg upon a Table, and with a Chopping-
knife, you must lay it open as broad as you can, then you must   20
take out the Bone, and beat the Flesh soundly with a rowling-
pin, then take Salt, Pepper, Cloves, Mace and Ginger, some
sweet Herbs, and season it very well, then rowl it up like
Brawn, and put it into the Oven for two Hours.

WOMAN. Heavens reward your Ladyship—I have two little   25
Babies too that are pitious bad with the Graips, an't please ye.

MRS SULLEN. Put a little Pepper and Salt in their Bellies,
good Woman. I beg your Ladyship's

Enter LADY BOUNTIFUL.

Pardon for taking your Business out of your Hands, I have been
a tampering here a little with one of your Patients.   30

LADY BOUNTIFUL. Come, good Woman, don't mind this mad
Creature, I am the Person that you want, I suppose—What
wou'd you have, Woman?

MRS SULLEN. She wants something for her Husband's sore
Leg.   35

LADY BOUNTIFUL. What's the matter with his Leg, Goody?

WOMAN. It come first, as one might say, with a sort of Dizziness
in his Foot, then he had a kind of a Laziness in his Joints, and
then his Leg broke out, and then it swell'd, and then it clos'd

again, and then it broke out again, and then it fester'd, and then it   40
grew better, and then it grew worse again.

MRS SULLEN. Ha, ha, ha.

LADY BOUNTIFUL. How can you be merry with the Misfortunes
of other People?

MRS SULLEN. Because my own make me sad, Madam.   45

LADY BOUNTIFUL. The worst Reason in the World, Daughter,
your own Misfortunes shou'd teach you to pitty others.

MRS SULLEN. But the Woman's Misfortunes and mine are
nothing alike, her Husband is sick, and mine, alas, is in Health.

LADY BOUNTIFUL. What! wou'd you wish your Husband sick?   50

MRS SULLEN. Not of a sore Leg, of all things.

LADY BOUNTIFUL. Well, good Woman, go to the Pantrey,
get your Belly-full of Victuals, then I'll give you a Receipt of Diet-
drink for your Husband—But d'ye hear Goody, you must not
let your Husband move too much.   55

WOMAN. No, no, Madam, the poor Man's inclinable enough to lye
still.

Exit

LADY BOUNTIFUL. Well, Daughter *Sullen*, tho' you laugh, I
have done Miracles about the Country here with my Receipts.

MRS. SULLEN. Miracles, indeed, if they have cur'd any Body,   60
but, I believe, Madam, the Patient's Faith goes farther toward
the Miracle than your Prescription.

LADY BOUNTIFUL. Fancy helps in some Cases, but there's your
Husband who has as little Fancy as any Body, I brought him
from Death's-door.   65

MRS SULLEN. I suppose, Madam, you made him drink plenti-
fully of Asse's Milk.

Enter DORINDA *runs to* MRS SULLEN.

DORINDA. News, dear Sister, news, news.

Enter ARCHER *running*.

ARCHER. Where, where is my Lady *Bountiful*—Pray which is
the old Lady of you three?   70

LADY BOUNTIFUL. I am.

ARCHER. O, Madam, the Fame of your Ladyship's Charity,
Goodness, Benevolence, Skill and Ability have drawn me hither

to implore your Ladyship's Help in behalf of my unfortunate
Master, who is this Moment breathing his last.   75

LADY BOUNTIFUL.   Your Master! where is he?

ARCHER.   At your Gate, Madam, drawn by the Appearance of
your handsome House to view it nearer, and walking up the
Avenue within five Paces of the Court-Yard, he was taken ill of
a sudden with a sort of I know not what, but down he fell, and   80
there he lies.

LADY BOUNTIFUL.   Here, *Scrub*, *Gipsey*, all run, get my easie
Chair down Stairs, put the Gentleman in it, and bring him in
quickly, quickly.

ARCHER.   Heaven will reward your Ladyship for this charitable   85
Act.

LADY BOUNTIFUL.   Is your Master us'd to these Fits?

ARCHER.   O yes, Madam, frequently—I have known him have
five or six of a Night.

LADY BOUNTIFUL.   What's his Name?   90

ARCHER.   Lord, Madam, he's a dying, a Minute's Care or Neglect
may save or destroy his Life.

LADY BOUNTIFUL.   Ah, poor Gentleman! come Friend, show
me the way, I'll see him brought in my self.

Exit with ARCHER.

DORINDA.   O Sister, my Heart flutters about strangely, I can   95
hardly forbear running to his Assistance.

MRS SULLEN.   And I'll lay my Life, he deserves your Assistance
more than he wants it; did not I tell you that my Lord wou'd
find a way to come at you. Love's his Distemper, and you must
be the Physitian; put on all your Charms, summon all your   100
Fire into your Eyes, plant the whole Artillery of your Looks
against his Breast, and down with him.

DORINDA.   O Sister, I'm but a young Gunner, I shall be afraid
to shoot, for fear the Piece shou'd recoil and hurt my self.

MRS SULLEN.   Never fear, you shall see me shoot before you,   105
if you will.

DORINDA.   No, no, dear Sister, you have miss'd your Mark so
unfortunately, that I shan't care for being instructed by you.

Enter AIMWELL *in a Chair, carry'd by* ARCHER *and* SCRUB,

LADY BOUNTIFUL, GIPSEY. AIMWELL *counterfeiting a Swoon.*

LADY BOUNTIFUL. Here, here, let's see the Hartshorn-drops—
   Gipsey a Glass of fair Water, his Fit's very strong—Bless me,   110
   how his Hands are clinch'd.

ARCHER. For shame, Ladies, what d'ye do? why don't you help
   us—Pray, Madam, [*To* DORINDA.] Take his Hand and open
   it if you can, whilst I hold his Head.

                                        DORINDA *takes his Hand.*

DORINDA. Poor, Gentleman,—Oh—he has got my Hand within   115
   his, and squeezes it unmercifully—

LADY BOUNTIFUL, 'Tis the Violence of his Convulsion, Child.

ARCHER. O, Madam, he's perfectly possess'd in these Cases—
   he'll bite if you don't have a care.

DORINDA. Oh, my Hand, my Hand.   120

LADY BOUNTIFUL. What's the matter with the foolish Girl? I
   have got this Hand open, you see, with a great deal of Ease.

ARCHER. Ay, but, Madam, your Daughter's Hand is somewhat
   warmer than your Ladyship's, and the Heat of it draws the
   Force of the Spirits that way.   125

MRS SULLEN. I find, Friend, you're very learned in these sorts
   of Fits.

ARCHER. 'Tis no wonder, Madam, for I'm often troubled with
   them my self, I find my self extreamly ill at this Minute.

                                Looking hard at MRS SULLEN.

MRS SULLEN. [*Aside.*] I fancy I cou'd find a way to cure you.   130

LADY BOUNTIFUL. His Fit holds him very long.

ARCHER. Longer than usual, Madam,—Pray, young Lady, open
   his breast and give him Air.

LADY BOUNTIFUL. Where did his illness take him first, pray?

ARCHER. To Day at Church, Madam.   135

LADY BOUNTIFUL. In what manner was he taken?

ARCHER. Very strangely, my Lady. He was of a sudden touch'd
   with something in his Eyes, which at the first he only felt, but
   cou'd not tell whether 'twas Pain or Pleasure.

LADY BOUNTIFUL. Wind, nothing but Wind.   140

ARCHER. By soft Degrees it grew and mounted to his Brain, there

his Fancy caught it; there form'd it so beautiful, and dress'd it
up in such gay pleasing Colours, that his transported Appetite
seized the fair Idea, and straight convey'd it to his Heart. That
hospitable Seat of Life sent all its sanguine Spirits forth to meet,　145
and open'd all its sluicy Gates to take the Stranger in.

LADY BOUNTIFUL.　Your Master should never go without a
Bottle to smell to—Oh!—He recovers—The Lavender Water—
Some Feathers to burn under his Nose—Hungary-water to rub
his Temples—O, he comes to himself. Hem a little, Sir, hem—　150
Gipsey, bring the Cordial-water.

⟨*Exit* GIPSEY⟩

AIMWELL *seems to awake in amaze.*

DORINDA.　How d'ye, Sir?
AIMWELL.　Where am I?

Rising.

Sure I have pass'd the Gulph of silent Death,
And now I land on the *Elisian* Shore—　　　　　　　155
Behold the Goddess of those happy Plains,
Fair *Proserpine*—Let me adore thy bright Divinity.

Kneels to DORINDA *and kisses her Hand.*

MRS SULLEN.　So, so, so, I knew where the Fit wou'd end.
AIMWELL.　*Euridice* perhaps—
　　How cou'd thy *Orpheus* keep his word,　　　　　160
　　And not look back upon thee;
　　No Treasure but thy self cou'd sure have brib'd him
　　To look one Minute off thee.
LADY BOUNTIFUL.　Delirious, poor Gentleman.
ARCHER.　Very Delirious, Madam, very Delirious.　　　165
AIMWELL.　*Martin*'s Voice, I think.
ARCHER.　Yes, my Lord—How do's your Lordship?
LADY BOUNTIFUL.　Lord! did you mind that, Girls.
AIMWELL.　Where am I?
ARCHER.　In very good Hands, Sir,—You were taken just now　170
　　with one of your old Fits under the Trees just by this good Lady's
　　House, her Ladyship had you taken in, and has miraculously
　　brought you to your self, as you see—
AIMWELL.　I am so confounded with Shame, Madam, that I can

now only beg Pardon—And refer my Acknowledgements for 175
your Ladyship's Care, till an Opportunity offers of making some
Amends—I dare be no longer troublesome—*Martin*, give two
Guineas to the Servants.

Going.

DORINDA. Sir, you may catch cold by going so soon into the
Air, you don't look, Sir, as if you were perfectly recover'd.   180

Here ARCHER *talks to* LADY BOUNTIFUL *in dumb shew.*

AIMWELL. That I shall never be, Madam, my present Illness is so
rooted, that I must expect to carry it to my Grave.

MRS SULLEN. Don't despair, Sir, I have known several in your
Distemper shake it off, with a Fortnight's Physick.

LADY BOUNTIFUL. Come, Sir, your Servant has been telling 185
me that you're apt to relapse if you go into the Air—Your good
Manners shan't get the better of ours—You shall sit down again,
Sir,—Come, Sir, we don't mind Ceremonies in the Country—
⟨*Enter* GIPSEY.⟩ Here, Sir, my service t'ye—You shall taste
my Water; 'tis a Coridal I can assure you, and of my own making 190
—drink it off, Sir, [AIMWELL *drinks.*] And how d'ye find your
self now, Sir.

AIMWELL. Somewhat better—Tho' very faint still.

LADY BOUNTIFUL. Ay, ay, People are always faint after these
Fits—Come Girls, you shall show the Gentleman the House, 'tis 195
but an old Family Building, Sir, but you had better walk about
and cool by Degrees than venture immediately into the Air—
You'll find some tolerable Pictures—*Dorinda*, show the
Gentleman the way. [*Exit.*] I must go to the poor Woman below.

DORINDA. This way, Sir.   200

AIMWELL. Ladies shall I beg leave for my Servant to wait on you,
for he understands Pictures very well.

MRS SULLEN. Sir, we understand Originals, as well as he do's
Pictures, so he may come along.

Exit DORINDA, MRS SULLEN, AIMWELL,
ARCHER ⟨, GIPSEY⟩. AIMWELL *leads* DORINDA.

Enter FOIGARD *and* SCRUB, *meeting.*

FOIGARD. Save you, Master *Scrub.*   205

SCRUB. Sir, I won't be sav'd your way—I hate a Priest, I abhor
the French, and I defie the Devil—Sir, I'm a bold *Briton* and will
spill the last drop of my Blood to keep out Popery and Slavery.

FOIGARD. Master *Scrub*, you wou'd put me down in Politicks,
and so I wou'd be speaking with Mrs. *Shipsey*.   210

SCRUB. Good Mr. Priest, you can't speak with her, she's sick, Sir,
she's gone abroad, Sir, she's—dead two Months ago, Sir.

Enter GIPSEY.

GIPSEY. How now, Impudence; how dare you talk so saucily to
the Doctor? Pray, Sir, don't take it ill; for the Common-people
of *England* are not so civil to Strangers, as—   215

SCRUB. You lie, you lie—'Tis the Common People that are
civilest to Strangers.

GIPSEY. Sirrah, I have a good mind to—Get you out, I say.

SCRUB. I won't.

GIPSEY. You won't, Sauce-box—Pray, Doctor, what is the   220
Captain's Name that came to your Inn last Night?

SCRUB. The Captain! Ah, the Devil, there she hampers me again;
—The Captain has me on one side, and the Priest on t'other:—
So between the Gown and the Sword, I have a fine time on't.—
But, *Cedunt Arma togae.*   225

Going.

GIPSEY. What, Sirrah, won't you march?

SCRUB. No, my Dear, I won't march—But I'll walk—
⟨*Aside*⟩ And I'll make bold to listen a little too.

Goes behind the side-Scene, and listens.

GIPSEY. Indeed, Doctor, the Count has been barbarously
treated, that's the Truth on't.   230

FOIGARD. Ah, Mrs. *Gipsey*, upon my Shoul, now, *Gra*, his
Complainings wou'd mollifie the Marrow in your Bones, and
move the Bowels of your Commiseration; he veeps, and he dances,
and he fistles, and he swears, and he laughs, and he stamps, and he
sings: In Conclusion, Joy, he's afflicted, *a la Francois*, and a 235
Stranger wou'd not know whider to cry, or to laugh with him.

GIPSEY. What wou'd you have me do, Doctor?

FOIGARD. Noting, Joy, but only hide the Count in Mrs. *Sullen*'s Closet when it is dark.

GIPSEY. Nothing! Is that Nothing? it wou'd be both a Sin and a 240 shame, Doctor.

FOIGARD. Here is twenty *Lewidores*, Joy, for your shame; and I will give you Absolution for the Shin.

GIPSEY. But won't that Money look like a Bribe?

FOIGARD. Dat is according as you shall tauk it.—If you 245 receive the Money beforehand, 'twill be *Logicè* a Bribe; but if you stay till afterwards, 'twill be only a Gratification.

GIPSEY. Well, Doctor, I'll take it *Logicè*.—But what must I do with my Conscience, Sir?

FOIGARD. Leave dat wid me, Joy; I am your Priest, *Gra*; and 250 your Conscience is under my Hands.

GIPSEY. But shou'd I put the Count into the Closet—

FOIGARD. Vel, is dere any Shin for a Man's being in a Closhet; one may go to Prayers in a Closhet.

GIPSEY. But if the Lady shou'd come into her Chamber, and go 255 to Bed?

FOIGARD. Vel, and is dere any Shin in going to Bed, Joy?

GIPSEY. Ay, but if the Parties shou'd meet, Doctor?

FOIGARD. Vel den—The Parties must be responsable.—Do you be after putting the Count in the Closet; and leave the Shins wid 260 themselves.—I will come with the Count to instruct you in your Chamber.

GIPSEY. Well, Doctor, your Religion is so pure—Methinks I'm so easie after an Absolution, and can sin afresh with so much security, that I'm resolved to die a Martyr to't.—Here's the Key 265 of the Garden-door, come in the back way when 'tis late,—I'll be ready to receive you; but don't so much as whisper, only take hold of my Hand, I'll lead you, and do you lead the Count, and follow me.

Exeunt.

Enter SCRUB.

SCRUB. What Witchcraft now have these two Imps of the Devil 270 been a hatching here?—There's twenty *Lewidores*, I heard that, and saw the Purse: But I must give room to my Betters.

Enter AIMWELL *leading* DORINDA, *and making Love in dumb*
Show—MRS SULLEN *and* ARCHER.

MRS SULLEN.   Pray, Sir, [*To* ARCHER] how d'ye like that Piece?
ARCHER.   O, 'tis *Leda.*—You find, Madam, how *Jupiter* comes
   disguis'd to make Love—   275
MRS SULLEN.   But what think you there of *Alexander's* Battles?
ARCHER.   We want only a *Le Brun*, Madam, to draw greater
   Battles, and a greater General of our own.—The *Danube*,
   Madam, wou'd make a greater Figure in a Picture than the
   Granicus; and we have our *Ramelies* to match their *Arbela*.   280
MRS SULLEN.   Pray, Sir, what Head is that in the Corner there?
ARCHER.   O, Madam, 'tis poor *Ovid* in his Exile.
MRS SULLEN.   What was he banish'd for?
ARCHER.   His ambitious Love, Madam. [*Bowing.*] His Misfortune
   touches me.   285
MRS SULLEN.   Was he successful in his Amours?
ARCHER.   There he has left us in the dark.—He was too much a
   Gentleman to tell.
MRS SULLEN.   If he were secret, I pity him.
ARCHER.   And if he were successful, I envy him.   290
MRS SULLEN.   How d'ye like that *Venus* over the Chimney?
ARCHER.   *Venus*! I protest, Madam, I took it for your Picture;
   but now I look again, 'tis not handsome enough.
MRS SULLEN.   Oh, what a Charm is Flattery! if you wou'd see
   my Picture, there it is, over that Cabinet;—How d'ye like it?   295
ARCHER.   I must admire any thing, Madam, that has the least
   Resemblance of you—But, methinks, Madam—[*He looks at the*
   Picture and MRS SULLEN *three or four times, by turns.*] Pray,
   Madam, who drew it?
MRS SULLEN.   A famous Hand, Sir.   300

Here AIMWELL *and* DORINDA *go off.*

ARCHER.   A famous Hand, Madam—Your Eyes, indeed, are
   featur'd there; but where's the sparkling Moisture, shining fluid,
   in which they swim. The Picture indeed has your Dimples; but
   where's the Swarm of killing *Cupids* that shou'd ambush there?
   the Lips too are figur'd out; but where's the Carnation Dew, the 305
   pouting Ripeness that tempts the Taste in the Original?

MRS SULLEN. ⟨*Aside.*⟩ Had it been my Lot to have match'd with
such a Man!

ARCHER. Your Breasts too, presumptous Man! what! paint
Heaven! *Apropo* Madam, in the very next Picture is *Salmoneus*, 310
that was struck dead with Lightning, for offering to imitate
Jove's Thunder; I hope you serv'd the Painter so, Madam?

MRS SULLEN. Had my Eyes the power of Thunder, they shou'd
employ their Lightning better.

ARCHER. There's the finest Bed in that Room, Madam, I suppose 315
'tis your Ladyship's Bed-Chamber.

⟨*Indicating another room.*⟩

MRS SULLEN. And what then, Sir?

ARCHER. I think that the Quilt is the richest that ever I saw:—I
can't at this Distance, Madam, distinguish the Figures of the
Embroidery; will you give me leave, Madam— 320

MRS SULLEN. ⟨*Aside.*⟩ The Devil take his Impudence.—Sure
if I gave him an opportunity, he durst not offer it.—I have a great
mind to try.—

Going.

Returns.

S'death, what am I doing?—And alone too!—Sister, Sister?

Runs out.

ARCHER. I'll follow her close— 325
For where a French-*man durst attempt to storm,*
A Briton *sure may well the* Work *perform.*

Going.

Enter SCRUB.

SCRUB. *Martin*, Brother *Martin.*

ARCHER. O, Brother *Scrub*, I beg your Pardon, I was not a going;
here's a Guinea, my Master order'd you. 330

SCRUB. A Guinea, hi, hi, hi, a Guinea! eh—by this Light it is a
Guinea; but I suppose you expect One and twenty Shillings in
change.

ARCHER. Not at all; I have another for *Gipsey*.

SCRUB. A Guinea for her! Faggot and Fire for the Witch.—Sir, 335
give me that Guinea, and I'll discover a Plot.

ARCHER. A Plot!

SCRUB. Ay, Sir, a Plot, and a horrid Plot.—First, it must be a
Plot because there's a Woman in't; secondly, it must be a Plot
because there's a Priest in't; thirdly, it must be a Plot because 340
there's *French* Gold in't; and fourthly, it must be a Plot, because
I don't know what to make on't.

ARCHER. Nor any body else, I'm afraid, Brother *Scrub*.

SCRUB. Truly I'm afraid so too; for where there's a Priest and a
Woman, there's always a Mystery and a Riddle.—This I know, 345
that here has been the Doctor with a Temptation in one Hand,
and an Absolution in the other; and *Gipsey* has sold her self to
the Devil; I saw the Price paid down, my Eyes shall take their
Oath on't.

ARCHER. And is all this bustle about *Gipsey*. 350

SCRUB. That's not all; I cou'd hear but a Word here and there;
but I remember they mention'd a Count, a Closet, a back Door,
and a Key.

ARCHER. The Count! did you hear nothing of Mrs. *Sullen?*

SCRUB. I did hear some word that sounded that way; but 355
whether it was *Sullen* or *Dorinda*, I cou'd not distinguish.

ARCHER. You have told this matter to no Body, Brother?

SCRUB. Told! No, Sir, I thank you for that; I'm resolv'd never
to speak one word *pro* nor *con*, till we have a Peace.

ARCHER. You're i'th right, Brother *Scrub*; here's a Treaty a foot 360
between the Count and the Lady.—The Priest and the Chambermaid are the Plenipotentiaries.—It shall go hard but I find a way
to be included in the Treaty.—Where's the Doctor now?

SCRUB. He and *Gipsey* are this moment devouring my Lady's
Marmalade in the Closet. 365

AIMWELL. [*From without.*] *Martin, Martin.*

ARCHER. I come, Sir, I come.

SCRUB. But you forget the other Guinea, Brother *Martin*.

ARCHER. Here, I give it with all my Heart.

SCRUB. And I take it with all my Soul. 370

Exeunt severally.

I'cod, I'll spoil your Plotting, Mrs. *Gipsey*; and if you shou'd
set the Captain upon me, these two Guineas will buy me off.

Exit.

Enter MRS SULLEN *and* DORINDA *meeting.*

MRS SULLEN. Well, Sister.

DORINDA. And well, Sister.

MRS SULLEN. What's become of my Lord? 375

DORINDA. What's become of his Servant?

MRS SULLEN. Servant! he's a prettier Fellow, and a finer Gentle-man by fifty Degrees than his Master.

DORINDA. O'my Conscience, I fancy you cou'd beg that Fellow at the Gallows-foot. 380

MRS SULLEN. O'my Conscience, I wou'd, provided I cou'd put a Friend of yours in his Room.

DORINDA. You desir'd me, Sister to leave you, when you trans-gress'd the Bounds of Honour.

MRS SULLEN. Thou dear censorious Country-Girl—What dost 385
mean? you can't think of the Man without the Bedfellow, I find.

ORINDA. I don't find any thing unnatural in that thought, while the Mind is conversant with Flesh and Blood, it must conform to the Humours of the Company.

MRS SULLEN. How a little Love and good Company improves 390
a Woman; why, Child, you begin to live—you never spoke before.

DORINDA. Because I was never spoke to.—My Lord has told me that I have more Wit and Beauty than any of my Sex; and truly I begin to think the Man is sincere. 395

MRS SULLEN. You're in the right, *Dorinda*, Pride is the Life of a Woman, and Flattery is our daily Bread; and she's a Fool that won't believe a Man there, as much as she that believes him in any thing else—But I'll lay you a Guinea, that I had finer things said to me than you had. 400

DORINDA. Done—What did your Fellow say to ye?

MRS SULLEN. My Fellow took the Picture of *Venus* for Mine.

DORINDA. But my Lover took me for *Venus* her self.

MRS SULLEN. Common Cant! had my Spark call'd me a *Venus* directly, I shou'd have believed him a Footman in good earnest. 405

DORINDA. But my Lover was upon his Knees to me.

MRS SULLEN And mine was upon his Tiptoes to me.

DORINDA. Mine vow'd to die for me.

MRS SULLEN. Mine swore to die with me.

DORINDA. Mine spoke the softest moving things.　410
MRS SULLEN. Mine had his moving things too.
DORINDA. Mine kiss'd my Hand Ten thousand times.
MRS SULLEN. Mine has all that Pleasure to come.
DORINDA. Mine offer'd Marriage.
MRS. SULLEN. O Lard! D'ye call that a moving thing?　415
DORINDA. The sharpest Arrow in his Quiver, my dear Sister,——
　Why, my Ten thousand Pounds may lie brooding here this
　seven Years, and hatch nothing at last but some ill natur'd
　Clown like yours:——Whereas, If I marry my Lord *Aimwell*, there
　will be Title, Place and Precedence, the Park, the Play, and the　420
　drawing-Room, Splendor, Equipage, Noise and Flambeaux——
　Hey, my Lady *Aimwell's* Servants there——Lights, Lights to the
　Stairs——My Lady *Aimwell's* Coach put forward——Stand by,
　make room for her Ladyship——Are not these things moving?——
　What! melancholly of a sudden?　425
MRS SULLEN. Happy, happy Sister! your Angel has been
　watchful for your Happiness, whilst mine has slept regardless of
　his Charge.——Long smiling Years of circling Joys for you, but
　not one Hour for me!

Weeps.

DORINDA. Come, my Dear, we'll talk of something else.　430
MRS SULLEN. O *Dorinda*, I own my self a Woman, full of my Sex,
　a gentle, generous Soul,——easie and yielding to soft Desires; a
　spacious Heart, where Love and all his Train might lodge. And
　must the fair Apartment of my Breast be made a Stable for a Brute
　to lie in?　435
DORINDA. Meaning your Husband, I suppose.
MRS SULLEN. Husband! no,——Even Husband is too soft a Name
　for him.——But, come, I expect my Brother here to Night or to
　Morrow; he was abroad when my Father marry'd me; perhaps
　he'll find a way to make me easy.　440
DORINDA. Will you promise not to make your self easy in the
　mean time with my Lord's Friend?
MRS SULLEN. You mistake me, Sister——It happens with us, as
　among the Men, the greatest Talkers are the Greatest Cowards;
　and there's a Reason for it; those Spirits evaporate in prattle,　445
　which might do more Mischief if they took another Course;——

Tho' to confess the Truth, I do love that Fellow;—And if I met him drest as he shou'd be, and I undrest as I shou'd be—Look'ye, Sister, I have no supernatural Gifts;—I can't swear I cou'd resist the Temptation,—tho' I can safely promise to avoid it; 450 and that's as much as the best of us can do.

Exit MRS SULLEN *and* DORINDA.

Enter AIMWELL *and* ARCHER *laughing.*

ARCHER. And the awkard Kindness of the good motherly old Gentlewoman—

AIMWELL. And the coming Easiness of the young one—S'death, 455 'tis pity to deceive her.

ARCHER. Nay, if you adhere to those Principles, stop where you are.

AIMWELL. I can't stop; for I love her to distraction.

ARCHER. S'death, if you love her a hair's breadth beyond discre- 460 tion, you must go no farther.

AIMWELL. Well, well, any thing to deliver us from sauntering away our idle Evenings at *White's*, *Tom's*, or *Will's* and be stinted to bear looking at our old Acquaintance, the Cards; because our impotent Pockets can't afford us a Guinea for the mercenary 465 Drabs.

ARCHER. Or be obliged to some Purse-proud Coxcomb for a scandalous Bottle, where we must not pretend to our share of the Discourse, because we can't pay our Club o'th Reckoning;— dam it, I had rather spunge upon *Morris*, and sup upon a Dish of 470 *Bohee* scor'd behind the Door.

AIMWELL. And there expose our want of Sense by talking Criti- cisms, as we shou'd our want of Money by railing at the Govern- ment.

ARCHER. Or be obliged to sneak into the side-Box, and between 475 both Houses steal two Acts of a Play, and because we han't Money to see the other three, we come away discontented, and damn the whole five.

AIMWELL. And Ten thousand such rascally Tricks,—had we out-liv'd our Fortunes among our Acquaintance.—But now— 480

ARCHER. Ay, now is the time to prevent all this.—Strike while the Iron is hot.—This Priest is the luckiest part of our Adventure; —He shall marry you, and pimp for me.

AIMWELL. But I shou'd not like a Woman that can be so fond of a *Frenchman*.   485

ARCHER. Alas, Sir, Necessity has no Law; the Lady may be in Distress; perhaps she has a confounded Husband, and her Revenge may carry her farther than her Love.—I gad, I have so good an Opinion of her, and of my self, that I begin to fancy strange things; and we must say this for the Honour of our   490 Women, and indeed of our selves, that they do stick to their Men, as they do to their *Magna Charta*.—If the Plot lies as I suspect,—I must put on the Gentleman.—But here comes the Doctor.—I shall be ready.

Exit.

Enter FOIGARD.

FOIGARD. Sauve you, noble Friend.   495

AIMWELL. O Sir, your Servant; pray Doctor, may I crave your Name?

FOIGARD. Fat Naam is upon me? my Naam is *Foigard*, Joy.

AIMWELL. *Foigard*, a very good Name for a Clergyman: Pray, Doctor *Foigard*, were you ever in *Ireland*?   500

FOIGARD. *Ireland*! No, Joy.—Fat sort of Plaace is dat saam *Ireland*? dey say de People are catcht dere when dey are young.

AIMWELL. And some of 'em when they're old;—as for Example.

Takes FOIGARD *by the Shoulder.*

Sir, I arrest you as a Traytor against the Government; you're a Subject of *England*, and this Morning shew'd me a Com-   505 mission, by which you serv'd as Chaplain in the *French* Army: This is Death by our Law, and your Reverence must hang for't.

FOIGARD. Upon my Shoul, Noble Friend, dis is strange News you tell me, Fader *Foigard* a Subject of *England*, de son of a *Burgo-master* of *Brussels*, a Subject of *England*! Ubooboo—   510

AIMWELL. The Son of a Bogtrotter in *Ireland*; Sir, your Tongue will condemn you before any Bench in the Kingdom.

FOIGARD. And is my Tongue all your Evidensh, Joy?

AIMWELL. That's enough.

FOIGARD. No, no, Joy, for I vill never spake *English* no more.   515

AIMWELL. Sir, I have other Evidence—Here, *Martin*, you know this Fellow.

Enter ARCHER.

ARCHER. [*In a Brogue.*] Saave you, my dear Cussen, how do's your Health?

FOIGARD. [*Aside.*] Ah! Upon my Shoul dere is my Countryman,   520
and his Brogue will hang mine. *Mynheer, Ick wet neat watt hey ʒacht, Ick universton ewe neat, sacramant.*

AIMWELL. Altering your Language won't do, Sir, this Fellow knows your Person, and will swear to your Face.

FOIGARD. Faace! fey, is dear a Brogue upon my Faash, too?   525

ARCHER. Upon my Soulvation dere ish Joy—But Cussen *Mackshane* vil you not put a remembrance upon me.

FOIGARD. [*Aside.*] *Mack-shane!* by St. *Paatrick*, dat is Naame, shure enough.

AIMWELL. I fancy *Archer*, you have it.   530

FOIGARD. The Devil hang you, Joy—By fat Acquaintance are you my Cussen.

ARCHER. O, de Devil hang your shelf, Joy, you know we were little Boys togeder upon de School, and your foster Moder's Son was marry'd upon my Nurse's Chister, Joy, and so we are Irish   535
Cussens.

FOIGARD. De Devil taak the Relation! vel, Joy, and fat School was it?

ARCHER. I tinks is vas—Aay—'Twas *Tipperary*.

FOIGARD. No, no, Joy, it vas *Kilkenny*.   540

AIMWELL. That's enough for us—Self-Confession—Come, Sir, we must deliver you into the Hands of the next Magistrate.

ARCHER. He sends you to Gaol, you're try'd next Assizes, and away you go swing into Purgatory.

FOIGARD. And is it so wid you, Cussen?   545

ARCHER. It vil be sho wid you, Cussen, if you don't immediately confess the Secret between you and Mrs. *Gipsey*—Look'e, Sir, the Gallows or the Secret, take your Choice.

FOIGARD. The Gallows! upon my Shoul I hate that saam Gallow, for it is a Diseash dat is fatal to our Family—Vel den, dere is   550
nothing, Shentlemens, but Mrs. *Shullen* wou'd spaak wid the

Count in her Chamber at Midnight, and dere is no Haarm, Joy, for I am to conduct the Count to the Plash, my shelf.

ARCHER. As I guess'd—Have you communicated the matter to the Count?   555

FOIGARD. I have not sheen him since.

ARCHER. Right agen; why then, Doctor,—you shall conduct me to the Lady instead of the Count.

FOIGARD. Fat my Cussen to the Lady! upon my Shoul, gra, dat is too much upon the Brogue.   560

ARCHER. Come, come, Doctor, consider we have got a Rope about your Neck, and if you offer to squeek, we'll stop your Wind-pipe, most certainly; we shall have another Job for you in a Day or two, I hope.

AIMWELL. Here's Company coming this way, let's into my   565
Chamber, and there concert our Affair farther.

ARCHER. Come, my dear Cussen, come along.

                                                         Exeunt.

Enter BONNIFACE, HOUNSLOW *and* BAGSHOT *at one Door,*
GIBBET *at the opposite.*

GIBBET. Well, Gentlemen, 'tis a fine Night for our Enterprise.

HOUNSLOW. Dark as Hell.

BAGSHOT. And blows like the Devil; our Landlord here has   570
show'd us the Window where we must break in, and tells us the
Plate stands in the Wainscoat Cupboard in the Parlour.

BONNIFACE. Ay, ay, Mr. *Bagshot*, as the saying is, Knives and
Forks, and Cups, and Canns, and Tumblers, and Tankards—
There's one Tankard, as the saying is, that's near upon as big as   575
me, it was a Present to the Squire from his Godmother, and
smells of Nutmeg and Toast like an *East India* Ship.

HOUNSLOW. Then you say we must divide at the Stair-head?

BONNIFACE. Yes, Mr. *Hounslow*, as the saying is—At one end
of the Gallery lies my Lady *Bountiful* and her Daughter, and   580
at the other Mrs. *Sullen*—As for the Squire—

GIBBET. He's safe enough, I have fairly enter'd him, and he's
more than half seas over already—But such a Parcel of Scoundrels
are got about him now, that I gad I was asham'd to be seen in
their Company.   585

BONNIFACE. 'Tis now Twelve, as the saying is—Gentlemen, you must set out at One.

GIBBET. *Hounslow*, do you and *Bagshot* see our Arms fix'd, and I'll come to you presently.

HOUNSLOW. }
BAGSHOT. } We will. 590

Exeunt.

GIBBET. Well, my dear *Bonny*, you assure me that *Scrub* is a Coward.

BONNIFACE. A Chicken, as the saying is—You'll have no Creature to deal with but the Ladies.

GIBBET. And I can assure you, Friend, there's a great deal of 595 Address and good Manners in robbing a Lady, I am the most a Gentleman that way that ever travell'd the Road—But, my dear Bonny, this Prize will be a Galleon, a *Vigo* Business—I warrant you we shall bring off three or four thousand Pound.

BONNIFACE. In Plate, Jewels and Money, as the saying is, you 600 may.

GIBBET. Why then, Tyburn, I defie thee, I'll get up to Town, sell off my Horse and Arms, buy my self some pretty Employment in the Household, and be as snug, and as honest as any Courtier of 'um all. 605

BONNIFACE. And what think you then of my Daughter *Cherry* for a Wife?

GIBBET. Look'ee, my dear *Bonny*—Cherry *is the Goddess I adore*, as the Song goes; but it is a Maxim that Man and Wife shou'd never have it in their Power to hang one another, for if they 610 should, the Lord have Mercy on 'um both.

Exeunt.

End of the Fourth Act.

ACT V

⟨SCENE I⟩

SCENE *continues. Knocking without.*

Enter BONNIFACE.

BONNIFACE.   Coming, coming—A Coach and six foaming
Horses at this time o'Night! Some great Man, as the saying is,
for he scorns to travel with other People.

Enter SIR CHARLES FREEMAN.

SIR CHARLES.   What, Fellow! a Publick-house, and a Bed when
other People Sleep.   5
BONNIFACE.   Sir, I an't a Bed, as the saying is.
SIR CHARLES.   Is Mr. *Sullen's* Family a Bed, think'e?
BONNIFACE.   All but the Squire himself, Sir, as the saying is,
he's in the House.
SIR CHARLES.   What Company has he?   10
BONNIFACE.   Why, Sir, there's the Constable, Mr. *Gage* the
Exciseman, the Hunchback'd-barber, and two or three other
Gentlemen.
SIR CHARLES.   I find my Sister's Letters gave me the true
Picture of her Spouse.   15

Enter SULLEN *drunk.*

BONNIFACE.   Sir, here's the Squire.
SULLEN.   The Puppies left me asleep—Sir.
SIR CHARLES. Well, Sir.
SULLEN.   Sir, I'm an unfortunate Man—I have three thousand
Pound a Year, and I can't get a Man to drink a Cup of Ale with   20
me.
SIR CHARLES.   That's very hard.
SULLEN.   Ay, Sir—And unless you have pitty upon me, and
smoke one Pipe with me, I must e'en go home to my Wife, and
I had rather go to the Devil by half.   25

SIR CHARLES. But, I presume, Sir, you won't see your Wife to Night, she'll be gone to Bed—you don't use to lye with your Wife in that Pickle?

SULLEN. What! not lye with my Wife! why, Sir, do you take me for an Atheist or a Rake.   30

SIR CHARLES. If you hate her, Sir, I think you had better lye from her.

SULLEN. I think so too, Friend—But I'm a Justice of Peace, and must do nothing against the Law.

SIR CHARLES. Law! as I take it, Mr. Justice, no Body observes   35
Law for Law's sake, only for the good of those for whom it was made.

SULLEN. But if the Law orders me to send you to Gaol, you must lye there, my Friend.

SIR CHARLES. Not unless I commit a Crime to deserve it.   40

SULLEN. A Crime! Oons an't I marry'd?

SIR CHARLES. Nay, Sir, if you call Marriage a Crime, you must disown it for a Law.

SULLEN. Eh!—I must be acquainted with you, Sir—But, Sir, I shou'd be very glad to know the Truth of this Matter.   45

SIR CHARLES. Truth, Sir, is a profound Sea, and few there be that dare wade deep enough to find out the bottom on't. Besides, Sir, I'm afraid the Line of your Understanding mayn't be long enough.

SULLEN. Look'e, Sir, I have nothing to say to your Sea of   50
Truth, but if a good Parcel of Land can intitle a Man to a little Truth, I have as much as any He in the Country.

BONNIFACE. I never heard your Worship, as the saying is, talk so much before.

SULLEN. Because I never met with a Man that I lik'd before—   55

BONNIFACE. Pray, Sir, as the saying is, let me ask you one Question, are not Man and Wife one Flesh?

SIR CHARLES. You and your Wife, Mr. Guts, may be one Flesh, because ye are nothing else—but rational Creatures have minds that must be united.   60

SULLEN. Minds.

SIR CHARLES. Ay, Minds, Sir, don't you think that the Mind takes place of the Body?

SULLEN. In some People.

SIR CHARLES. Then the Interest of the Master must be consulted 65
before that of his Servant.

SULLEN. Sir, you shall dine with me to Morrow.—Oons I
always thought that we were naturally one.

SIR CHARLES. Sir, I know that my two Hands are naturally one,
because they love one another, kiss one another, help one another 70
in all the Actions of Life, but I cou'd not say so much, if they
were always at Cuffs.

SULLEN. Then 'tis plain that we are two.

SIR CHARLES. Why don't you part with her, Sir?

SULLEN. Will you take her, Sir? 75

SIR CHARLES. With all my Heart.

SULLEN. You shall have her to Morrow Morning, and a Venison-
pasty into the Bargain.

SIR CHARLES. You'll let me have her Fortune too?

SULLEN. Fortune! why, Sir, I have no Quarrel at her Fortune— 80
I only hate the Woman, Sir, and none but the Woman shall
go.

SIR CHARLES. But her Fortune, Sir—

SULLEN. Can you play at Whisk, Sir?

SIR CHARLES. No, truly, Sir. 85

SULLEN. Nor at All-fours.

SIR CHARLES. Neither!

SULLEN. [*Aside.*] Oons! where was this Man bred. ⟨*To him.*⟩
Burn me, Sir, I can't go home, 'tis but two a Clock.

SIR CHARLES. For half an Hour, Sir, if you please—But you 90
must consider 'tis late.

SULLEN. Late! that's the Reason I can't go to Bed—Come,
Sir.—

　　　　　　　　　　　　　　　　　　　　　Exeunt.

Enter CHERRY, *runs across the Stage and knocks at* AIMWELL'S
Chamber-door. Enter AIMWELL *in his Night-cap and Gown.*

AIMWELL. What's the matter, you tremble, Child, you're frighted.

CHERRY. No wonder, Sir—But in short, Sir, this very Minute 95
a Gang of Rogues are gone to rob my Lady *Bountiful's* House.

AIMWELL. How!

D

CHERRY. I dogg'd 'em to the very Door, and left 'em breaking in.

AIMWELL. Have you alarm'd any Body else with the News.   100

CHERRY. No, no, Sir, I wanted to have discover'd the whole Plot, and twenty other things to your Man *Martin*; but I have search'd the whole House and can't find him; where is he?

AIMWELL. No matter, Child, will you guide me immediately to the House?   105

CHERRY. With all my Heart, Sir, my Lady *Bountiful* is my God-mother; and I love Mrs. *Dorinda* so well—

AIMWELL. *Dorinda*! The Name inspires me, the Glory and the Danger shall be all my own—Come, my Life, let me but get my Sword.   110

Exeunt.

⟨SCENE II⟩

SCENE, *Changes to a Bed-chamber in* LADY BOUNTIFUL'S *House.*

Enter MRS SULLEN, DORINDA *undress'd, a Table and Lights.*

DORINDA. 'Tis very late, Sister, no News of your Spouse yet?

MRS SULLEN. No, I'm condemned to be alone till towards four, and then perhaps I may be executed with his Company.

DORINDA. Well, my Dear, I'll leave you to your rest; you'll go directly to Bed, I suppose.   5

MRS SULLEN. I don't know what to do; hey-hoe!

DORINDA. That's a desiring Sigh, Sister.

MRS SULLEN. This is a languishing Hour, Sister.

DORINDA. And might prove a Critical Minute, if the pretty Fellow were here.   10

MRS SULLEN. Here! what, in my Bed-chamber, at two a Clock o'th Morning, I undress'd, the Family asleep, my hated Husband abroad, and my lovely Fellow at my Feet—O gad, Sister!

DORINDA. Thoughts are free, Sister, and them I allow you—So, my Dear, good Night.   15

MRS SULLEN. A good Rest to my dear *Dorinda* ⟨*Exit* DORINDA.⟩—Thoughts free! are they so? why then suppose him here, dress'd like a youthful, gay and burning Bridegroom.

[*Here* ARCHER *steals out of the Closet.*] with Tongue enchanting,
Eyes bewitching, Knees imploring. [*Turns a little o' one side,*   20
and sees ARCHER *in the Posture she describes.*] Ah! [*Shreeks, and*
runs to the other Side of the Stage] Have my Thoughts rais'd a
Spirit—What are you, Sir, a Man, or a Devil?
ARCHER. A Man, a Man, Madam.
MRS SULLEN. How shall I be sure of it?   25
ARCHER. Madam, I'll give you Demonstration this Minute.

Takes her hand.

MRS SULLEN. What, Sir! do you intend to be rude?
ARCHER. Yes, Madam, if you please.
MRS SULLEN. In the Name of Wonder, whence came ye?
ARCHER. From the Skies, Madam—I'm a *Jupiter* in Love, and   30
you shall be my *Alcmena*.
MRS SULLEN. How came you in?
ARCHER. I flew in at the Window, Madam, your Cozen *Cupid*
lent me his Wings, and your Sister *Venus* open'd the Casement.
MRS SULLEN. I'm struck dumb with Admiration.   35
ARCHER. And I with wonder.

Looks passionately at her.

MRS SULLEN. What will become of me?
ARCHER. How beautiful she looks—The teeming Jolly Spring
Smiles in her blooming Face, and when she was conceiv'd, her
Mother smelt to Roses, look'd on Lilies—   40

Lillies unfold their white, their fragrant Charms,
When the warm Sun thus Darts into their Arms.

Runs to her.

MRS SULLEN. [*Shreeks.*] Ah!
ARCHER. Oons, Madam, what d'ye mean? you'll raise the House.
MRS SULLEN. Sir, I'll wake the Dead before I bear this—What!   45
approach me with the Freedoms of a Keeper; I'm glad on't, your
Impudence has cur'd me.
ARCHER. If this be Impudence [*Kneels*] I leave to your partial
self; no panting Pilgrim after a tedious, painful Voyage, e'er
bow'd before his Saint with more Devotion.   50

v. ii. 31. Alcmena] 1707², c, w; Alimena 1707.

MRS SULLEN. [*Aside.*] Now, now, I'm ruined, if he kneels! ⟨*To him*⟩ rise thou prostrate Ingineer, not all thy undermining Skill shall reach my Heart—Rise, and know, I am a Woman without my Sex, I can love to all the Tenderness of Wishes, Sighs and Tears—But go no farther—Still to convince you that 55
I'm more than Woman, I can speak my Frailty, confess my Weakness even for you—But—

ARCHER. For me!

> *Going to lay hold on her.*

MRS SULLEN. Hold, Sir, build not upon that—For my most mortal hatred follows if you disobey what I command you 60
now—leave me this Minute—[*Aside*] If he denies, I'm lost.

ARCHER. Then you'll promise—

MRS SULLEN. Any thing another time.

ARCHER. When shall I come?

MRS SULLEN. To Morrow when you will. 65

ARCHER. Your Lips must seal the Promise.

MRS SULLEN. Pshaw!

ARCHER. They must, they must [*Kisses her*] Raptures and Paradice! and why not now, my Angel? the Time, the Place, Silence and Secrecy, all conspire—And the now conscious Stars 70
have preordain'd this Moment for my Happiness.

> *Takes her in his Arms.*

MRS SULLEN. You will not, cannot sure.

ARCHER. If the Sun rides fast, and disappoints not Mortals of to Morrow's Dawn, this Night shall crown my Joys.

MRS SULLEN. My Sex's Pride assist me. 75

ARCHER. My Sex's Strength help me.

MRS SULLEN. You shall kill me first.

ARCHER. I'll dye with you.

> *Carrying her off.*

MRS SULLEN. Thieves, Thieves, Murther—

Enter SCRUB *in his Breeches, and one Shoe.*

SCRUB. Thieves, Thieves, Murther, Popery. 80

ARCHER. Ha! the very timorous Stag will kill in rutting time.

> *Draws and offers to Stab* SCRUB.

SCRUB. [*Kneeling*] O, Pray, Sir, spare all I have and take my
  Life.

MRS SULLEN.   [*Holding* ARCHER'S *Hand.*] What do's the
  Fellow mean?   85

SCRUB. O, Madam, down upon your Knees, your Marrow-bones
  —He's one of 'um.

ARCHER. Of whom?

SCRUB. One of the Rogues—I beg your Pardon, Sir, one of the
  honest Gentlemen that just now are broke into the House.   90

ARCHER. How!

MRS SULLEN. I hope, you did not come to rob me?

ARCHER. Indeed I did, Madam, but I wou'd have taken nothing
  but what you might ha' spar'd, but your crying Thieves has
  wak'd this dreaming Fool, and so he takes 'em for granted.   95

SCRUB. Granted! 'tis granted, Sir, take all we have.

MRS SULLEN. The Fellow looks as if he were broke out of
  Bedlam.

SCRUB. Oons, Madam, they're broke in to the House with Fire
  and Sword, I saw them, heard them, they'll be here this Minute.   100

ARCHER. What, Thieves!

SCRUB. Under Favour, Sir, I think so.

MRS SULLEN. What shall we do, Sir?

ARCHER. Madam, I wish your Ladyship a good Night.

MRS SULLEN. Will you leave me?   105

ARCHER. Leave you! Lord, Madam, did you not command me
  to be gone just now upon pain of your immortal Hatred.

MRS SULLEN. Nay, but pray, Sir—

                                        Takes hold of him.

ARCHER. Ha, ha, ha, now comes my turn to be ravish'd.—You
  see now, Madam, you must use Men one way or other; but take   110
  this by the way, good Madam, that none but a Fool will give you
  the benefit of his Courage, unless you'll take his Love along
  with it.—How are they arm'd, Friend?

SCRUB. With Sword and Pistol, Sir.

ARCHER. Hush—I see a dark Lanthorn coming thro' the   115
  Gallery.—Madam, be assur'd I will protect you, or lose my Life.

MRS SULLEN. Your Life! no, Sir, they can rob me of nothing

that I value half so much; therefore, now, Sir let me intreat you
to be gone.

ARCHER. No, Madam, I'll consult my own Safety for the sake of 120
yours, I'll work by Stratagem: Have you Courage enough to
stand the appearance of 'em.

MRS SULLEN. Yes, yes, since I have scap'd your Hands, I can
face any thing.

ARCHER. Come hither, Brother *Scrub*, don't you know me? 125

SCRUB. Eh! my dear Brother, let me kiss thee.

Kisses ARCHER.

ARCHER. This way—Here—

ARCHER and SCRUB *hide behind the Bed.*

Enter GIBBET *with a dark Lanthorn in one Hand and a Pistol in
t'other.*

GIBBET. Ay, ay, this is the Chamber, and the Lady alone.

MRS SULLEN. Who are you, Sir? what wou'd you have? d'ye
come to rob me? 130

GIBBET. Rob you! alack a day, Madam, I'm only a younger
Brother; Madam; and so, Madam, if you make a Noise, I'll
shoot you thro' the Head; but don't be afraid, Madam.

Laying his Lanthorn and Pistol upon the Table.

These Rings, Madam, don't be concerned, Madam, I have a
profound Respect for you, Madam; your Keys, Madam, don't 135
be frighted, Madam, I'm the most of a Gentleman.
[*Searching her Pockets*] This Necklace, Madam, I never was
rude to a Lady;—I have a Veneration—for this Necklace—

Here ARCHER *having come round and seiz'd the
Pistols, takes* GIBBET *by the Collar, trips up his
Heels, and claps the Pistol to his Breast.*

ARCHER. Hold, profane Villain, and take the Reward of thy
Sacrilege. 140

GIBBET. Oh! Pray, Sir, don't kill me; I an't prepar'd.

ARCHER. How many is there of 'em, *Scrub*?

SCRUB. Five and Forty, Sir.

ARCHER. Then I must kill the Villain to have him out of the way.

GIBBET. Hold, hold, Sir, we are but three upon my Honour.   145
ARCHER. *Scrub*, will you undertake to secure him?
SCRUB. Not I, Sir; kill him, kill him.
ARCHER. Run to *Gipsey's* Chamber, there you'll find the
Doctor; bring him hither presently.

Exit SCRUB *running.*

Come, Rogue, if you have a short Prayer, say it.   150
GIBBET. Sir, I have no Prayer at all; the Government has pro-
vided a Chaplain to say Prayers for us on these Occasions.
MRS SULLEN. Pray, Sir, don't kill him;—You fright me as
much as him.
ARCHER. The Dog shall die, Madam, for being the Occasion of   155
my disappointment.—Sirrah, this Moment is your last.
GIBBET. Sir, I'll give you Two hundred Pound to spare my Life.
ARCHER. Have you no more, Rascal?
GIBBET. Yes, Sir, I can command Four hundred; but I must
reserve Two of 'em to save my Life at the Sessions.   160

Enter SCRUB *and* FOIGARD.

ARCHER. Here, Doctor, I suppose *Scrub* and you between you
may manage him.—Lay hold of him, Doctor.

FOIGARD *lays hold of* GIBBET.

GIBBET. What! turn'd over to the Priest already.—Look'ye,
Doctor, you come before your time; I'ant condemn'd yet, I
thank'ye.   165
FOIGARD. Come, my dear Joy, I vill secure your Body and your
Shoul too; I vill make you a good Catholick, and give you an
Absolution.
GIBBET. Absolution! can you procure me a Pardon, Doctor?
FOIGARD. No, Joy.—   170
GIBBET. Then you and your Absolution may go to the Devil.
ARCHER. Convey him into the Cellar, there bind him:—Take the
Pistol, and if he offers to resist, shoot him thro' the Head,—and
come back to us with all the speed you can.
SCRUB. Ay, ay, come, Doctor, do you hold him fast, and I'll   175
guard him.

⟨*Exeunt* SCRUB, FOIGARD *and* GIBBET.⟩

MRS SULLEN. But how came the Doctor?

ARCHER. In short, Madam—[*Shreeking without.*] S'death! the
Rogues are at work with the other Ladies.—I'm vex'd I parted
with the Pistol; but I must fly to their Assistance.—Will you stay   180
here, Madam, or venture your self with me.

MRS SULLEN. O, with you, dear Sir, with you.

Takes him by the Arm and Exeunt.

⟨SCENE III⟩

SCENE, *Changes to another Apartment in the same House.*

Enter HOUNSLOW *dragging in* LADY BOUNTIFUL, *and*
BAGSHOT *halling in* DORINDA; *the Rogues with Swords drawn.*

HOUNSLOW. Come, come, your Jewels, Mistriss.

BAGSHOT. Your Keys, your Keys, old Gentlewomen.

Enter AIMWELL *and* CHERRY.

AIMWELL. Turn this way, Villains; I durst engage an Army in
such a Cause.

He engages 'em both.

DORINDA. O, Madam, had I but a Sword to help the brave Man?   5

LADY BOUNTIFUL. There's three or four hanging up in the Hall;
but they won't draw. I'll go fetch one however.

Exit.

Enter ARCHER *and* MRS SULLEN.

ARCHER. Hold, hold, my Lord, every Man his Bird, pray.

They engage Man to Man, the Rogues are thrown and disarm'd.

CHERRY. What! the Rogues taken! then they'll impeach my
Father; I must give him timely Notice.   10

Runs out.

ARCHER. Shall we kill the Rogues?

AIMWELL. No, no, we'll bind them.

ARCHER. Ay, ay; [*To* MRS SULLEN *who stands by him.*] here,
Madam, lend me your Garter?

MRS SULLEN. The Devil's in this Fellow; he fights, loves, and 15
banters, all in a Breath.—Here's a Cord that the Rogues
brought with 'em, I suppose.

ARCHER. Right, right, the Rogue's Destiny, a Rope to hang
himself.—Come, my Lord,—This is but a scandalous sort of an
Office, [*Binding the Rogues together.*] if our Adventures shou'd 20
end in this sort of Hangman-work; but I hope there is something in prospect that—

Enter SCRUB.

Well, *Scrub*, have you secur'd your *Tartar*?

SCRUB. Yes, Sir, I left the Priest and him disputing about Religion.

AIMWELL. And pray carry these Gentlemen to reap the Benefit of 25
the Controversy.

Delivers the Prisoners to SCRUB, *who leads 'em out.*

MRS SULLEN. Pray, Sister, how came my Lord here?

DORINDA. And pray, how came the Gentleman here?

MRS SULLEN. I'll tell you the greatest piece of Villainy—

They talk in dumb show.

AIMWELL. I fancy, *Archer*, you have been more successful in 30
your Adventures than the House-breakers.

ARCHER. No matter for my Adventure, yours is the principal.—
Press her this Minute to marry you,—now while she's hurry'd
between the Palpitation of her Fear, and the Joy of her Deliverance, now while the Tide of her Spirits are at High-flood—Throw 35
your self at her Feet; speak some *Romantick* Nonsence or other;
—Address her like *Alexander* in the height of his Victory, con-
found her Senses, bear down her Reason, and away with her—
The Priest is now in the Cellar, and dare not refuse to do the work.

Enter LADY BOUNTIFUL.

AIMWELL. But how shall I get off without being observ'd? 40

ARCHER. You a Lover! and not find a way to get off—Let me
see.

AIMWELL. You bleed, *Archer*.

ARCHER. S'death, I'm glad on't; this Wound will do the Business

E

—I'll amuse the old Lady and Mrs. *Sullen* about dressing my   45
Wound, while you carry off *Dorinda*.

LADY BOUNTIFUL. Gentlemen, cou'd we understand how you
wou'd be gratified for the Services—

ARCHER. Come, come, my Lady, this is no time for Complements,
I'm wounded, Madam.   50

LADY BOUNTIFUL. } How! wounded!
MRS SULLEN.

DORINDA. I hope, Sir, you have received no Hurt?

AIMWELL. None, but what you may cure.—

Makes Love in dumb show.

LADY BOUNTIFUL. Let me see your Arm, Sir.—I must have
some Powder-sugar to stop the Blood—O me! an ugly Gash   55
upon my Word, Sir, you must go into Bed.

ARCHER. Ay, my Lady, a Bed wou'd do very well.—Madam,
[*To* MRS SULLEN.] Will you do me the Favour to conduct me
to a Chamber?

LADY BOUNTIFUL. Do, do, Daughter—while I get the Lint and   60
the Probe and the Plaister ready.

Runs out one way, AIMWELL *carries off* DORINDA
another.

ARCHER. Come, Madam, why don't you obey your Mother's
Commands.

MRS SULLEN. How can you, after what is past, have the Confidence to ask me?   65

ARCHER. And if you go to that, how can you after what is past,
have the Confidence to deny me?—Was not this Blood shed
in your Defence, and my Life expos'd for your Protection.—
Look'ye, Madam, I'm none of your *Romantick* Fools, that fight
Gyants and Monsters for nothing; my Valour is down right   70
Swiss; I'm a Soldier of Fortune and must be paid.

MRS SULLEN. 'Tis ungenerous in you, Sir, to upbraid me with
your Services.

ARCHER. 'Tis ungenerous in you, Madam, not to reward 'em.

MRS SULLEN. How! at the Expence of my Honour.   75

ARCHER. Honour! can Honour consist with Ingratitude? if you

wou'd deal like a Woman of Honour, do like a Man of Honour,
d'ye think I wou'd deny you in such a Case?

Enter a Servant.

SERVANT. Madam, my Lady order'd me to tell you that your
    Brother is below at the Gate.   80
MRS SULLEN. My Brother? Heavens be prais'd.—Sir, he shall
    thank you for your Services, he has it in his Power.
ARCHER. Who is your Brother, Madam?
MRS SULLEN. Sir *Charles Freeman.*—You'll excuse me, Sir; I
    must go and receive him.   85
ARCHER. Sir *Charles Freeman*! S'death and Hell!—My old
    Acquaintance. Now unless *Aimwell* has made good use of his
    time, all our fair Machine goes souse into the Sea like the *Edistone.*

                                                         Exit.

                        ⟨SCENE IV⟩

        SCENE, *Changes to the Gallery in the Same House.*

                Enter AIMWELL *and* DORINDA.

DORINDA. Well, well, my Lord, you have conquer'd; your late
    generous Action will, I hope, plead for my easie yielding, tho'
    I must own your Lordship had a Friend in the Fort before.
AIMWELL. The Sweete of *Hybla* dwell upon her Tongue.—
    Here, Doctor—   5

Enter FOIGARD *with a Book*

FOIGARD. Are you prepar'd boat?
DORINDA. I'm ready: But, first, my Lord one Word;—I have
    a frightful Example of a hasty Marriage in my own Family;
    when I reflect upon't, it shocks me. Pray, my Lord, consider a
    little—   10
AIMWELL. Consider! Do you doubt my Honour or my Love?
DORINDA. Neither: I do believe you equally Just as Brave.—
    And were your whole Sex drawn out for me to chuse, I shou'd
    not cast a look upon the Multitude if you were absent.—But

my Lord, I'm a Woman; Colours, Concealments may hide a   1
thousand Faults in me;—Therefore know me better first; I
hardly dare affirm I know my self in any thing except my Love.

AIMWELL. [*Aside.*] Such Goodness who cou'd injure; I find my
self unequal to the Task of Villain; she has gain'd my Soul, and
made it honest like her own;—I cannot, cannot hurt her. ⟨*To*   2
FOIGARD.⟩ Doctor, retire.

                         Exit FOIGARD.

Madam, behold your Lover and your Proselite, and judge of my
Passion by my Conversion.—I'm all a Lie, nor dare I give
Fiction to your Arms; I'm all Counterfeit except my Passion.

DORINDA. Forbid it Heaven! a Counterfeit!   2

AIMWELL. I am no Lord, but a poor needy Man, come with a
mean, a scandalous Design to prey upon your Fortune:—But
the Beauties of your Mind and Person have so won me from my
self, that like a trusty Servant, I prefer the Interest of my Mistress
to my own.   3

DORINDA. Sure I have had the Dream of some poor Mariner, a
sleepy image of a welcome Port, and wake involv'd in Storms.
—Pray, Sir, who are you?

AIMWELL. Brother to the Man whose Title I usurp'd, but
Stranger to his Honour or his Fortune.   3

DORINDA. Matchless Honesty—Once I was proud, Sir, of your
Wealth and Title, but now am prouder that you want it: Now
I can shew my Love was justly levell'd, and had no Aim but
Love. Doctor, come in.

Enter FOIGARD *at one Door*, GIPSEY *at another, who whispers*
DORINDA.

Your Pardon, Sir, we shall not want you now, Sir? you must   4
excuse me,—I'll wait on you presently.

                         Exit with GIPSEY.

FOIGARD. Upon my Shoul, now, dis is foolish.
                                    Exit.

---

v. IV. 40. Sir, we shall not want you now, Sir?] 1707[2]; Sir, we shannot; won'
you now, Sir? 1707; Sir, we sha'not; won't you now, Sir? c, w. This shoul
perhaps read: "We shannot want you now, Sir".

AIMWELL. Gone! and bid the Priest depart.—It has an ominous
  Look.

Enter ARCHER.

ARCHER. Courage, *Tom*—Shall I wish you Joy?   45
AIMWELL. No.
ARCHER. Oons, Man, what ha' you been doing?
AIMWELL. O, *Archer*, my Honesty, I fear has ruin'd me.
ARCHER. How!
AIMWELL. I have discover'd my self.   50
ARCHER. Discover'd! and without my Consent? what! have I
  embark'd my small Remains in the same bottom with yours, and
  you dispo'se of all without my Partnership?
AIMWELL. O, *Archer*, I own my Fault.
ARCHER. After Conviction—'Tis then too late for Pardon.—   55
  You may remember, Mr. *Aimwell*, that you propos'd this
  Folly—As you begun, so end it.—Henceforth I'll hunt my
  Fortune single.—So farewel.
AIMWELL. Stay, my dear *Archer*, but a Minute.
ARCHER. Stay! what to be despis'd, expos'd and laugh'd at—No,   60
  I wou'd sooner change Conditions with the worst of the Rogues
  we just now bound, than bear one scornful Smile from the proud
  Knight that once I treated as my equal.
AIMWELL. What Knight?
ARCHER. Sir *Charles Freeman*, Brother to the Lady that I had   65
  almost—But no matter for that, 'tis a cursed Night's Work, and
  so I leave you to make your best on't.

                                                            Going.

AIMWELL. *Freeman!*—One Word, *Archer*. Still I have Hopes;
  methought she receiv'd my Confession with Pleasure.
ARCHER. S'death! who doubts it?   70
AIMWELL. She consented after to the Match; and still I dare
  believe she will be just.
ARCHER. To her self, I warrant her, as you shou'd have been.
AIMWELL. By all my Hopes, she comes, and smiling comes.

Enter DORINDA *mighty gay.*

DORINDA. Come, my dear Lord,—I fly with Impatience to   75

your Arms.—The Minutes of my Absence was a tedious Year.
Where's this tedious Priest?

Enter FOIGARD.

ARCHER. Oons, a brave Girl.

DORINDA. I suppose, my Lord, this Gentleman is privy to our
Affairs?

ARCHER. Yes, yes, Madam, I'm to be your Father.

DORINDA. Come, Priest, do your Office.

ARCHER. Make hast, make hast, couple 'em any way. [*Takes
AIMWELL's Hand.*] Come, Madam, I'm to give you—

DORINDA. My Mind's alter'd, I won't.

ARCHER. Eh—

AIMWELL. I'm confounded.

FOIGARD. Upon my Shoul, and sho is my shelf.

ARCHER. What's the matter now, Madam?

DORINDA. Look'ye, Sir, one generous Action deserves another
—This Gentleman's Honour oblig'd him to hide nothing from
me; my Justice engages me to conceal nothing from him: In short,
Sir, you are the Person that you thought you counterfeited;
you are the true Lord Viscount *Aimwell*; and I wish your Lordship Joy. Now, Priest, you may be gone; if my Lord is pleas'd
now with the Match, let his Lordship marry me in the face of the
World.

AIMWELL. ARCHER. What do's she mean?

DORINDA. Here's a Witness for my Truth.

Enter SIR CHARLES *and* MRS SULLEN.

SIR CHARLES. My dear Lord *Aimwell*, I wish you Joy.

AIMWELL. Of what?

SIR CHARLES. Of your Honour and Estate: Your Brother died
the Day before I left *London*; and all your Friends have writ
after you to *Brussels*; among the rest I did my self the Honour.

ARCHER. Hark'ye, Sir Knight, don't you banter now?

SIR CHARLES. 'Tis Truth upon my Honour.

AIMWELL. Thanks to the pregnant Stars that form'd this
Accident.

ARCHER. Thanks to the Womb of Time that brought it forth;
away with it.

AIMWELL. Thanks to my Guardian Angel that led me to the Prize—

Taking DORINDA'S *Hand.*

ARCHER. And double Thanks to the noble Sir *Charles Freeman.* My Lord, I wish you Joy. My Lady I wish you Joy.—I Gad, Sir *Freeman,* you're the honestest Fellow living.—S'death, I'm grown strange airy upon this matter—My Lord, how d'ye?—a word, my Lord; don't you remember something of a previous Agreement, that entitles me to the Moyety of this Lady's Fortune, which, I think will amount to Five thousand Pound.

AIMWELL. Not a Penny, *Archer;* You wou'd ha' cut my Throat just now, because I wou'd not deceive this Lady.

ARCHER. Ay, and I'll cut your Throat again, if you shou'd deceive her now.

AIMWELL. That's what I expected; and to end the Dispute, the Lady's Fortune is Ten thousand Pound; we'll divide Stakes; take the Ten thousand Pound, or the Lady.

DORINDA. How! is your Lordship so indifferent?

ARCHER. No, no, no, Madam, his Lordship knows very well, that I'll take the Money; I leave you to his Lordship, and so we're both provided for.

Enter COUNT BELLAIR.

COUNT. *Mesdames, et Messieurs,* I am your Servant trice humble: I hear you be rob, here.

AIMWELL. The Ladies have been in some danger, Sir.

COUNT. And Begar, our Inn be rob too.

AIMWELL. Our Inn! by whom?

COUNT. By the Landlord, begar—Garzoon he has rob himself and run away.

ARCHER. Rob'd himself!

COUNT. Ay, begar, and me too of a hundre Pound.

ARCHER. A hundred Pound.

COUNT. Yes, that I ow'd him.

AIMWELL. Our Money's gone, *Frank.*

ARCHER. Rot the Money, my Wench is gone—*Scavez vous quelque chose de Madamoiselle Cherry?*

Enter a FELLOW *with a strong Box and a Letter.*

FELLOW. Is there one *Martin* here?

ARCHER. Ay, ay,—who wants him?

FELLOW. I have a Box here and Letter for him.

ARCHER. [*Taking the Box.*] Ha, ha, ha, what's here? *Legerde-*
main! by this Light, my Lord, our Money again; but this unfolds
the Riddle. [*Opening the Letter, reads.*] Hum, hum, hum—O,   150
'tis for the Publick good, and must be communicated to the
Company.

Mr. MARTIN,

My Father being afraid of an Impeachment by the Rogues that are
taken to Night is gone off, but if you can procure him a Pardon he   155
will maake great Discoveries that may be useful to the Country;
cou'd I have met you instead of your Master to Night, I wou'd have
deliver'd my self into your Hands with a Sum that much exceeds that
in your strong Box, which I have sent you, with an Assurance to my
dear Martin, *that I shall ever be his most faithful Friend till Death.*   160

CHERRY BONNIFACE.

there's a Billet-doux for you—As for the Father I think he
ought to be encouraged, and for the Daughter,—Pray, my
Lord, persuade your Bride to take her into her Service instead
of *Gipsey.*   165

AIMWELL. I can assure you, Madam, your Deliverance was owing
to her Discovery.

DORINDA. Your Command, my Lord, will do without the Obli-
gation. I'll take care of her.

SIR CHARLES. This good Company meets opportunely in favour   170
of a Design I have in behalf of my unfortunate Sister, I intend to
part from her Husband—Gentlemen will you assist me?

ARCHER. Assist you! S'death who wou'd not.

COUNT. Assist! Garzoon, we all assist.

Enter SULLEN.

SULLEN. What's all this?—They tell me Spouse that you had like   175
to have been rob'd.

MRS SULLEN. Truly, Spouse, I was pretty near it—Had not these
two Gentlemen interpos'd.

SULLEN. How came these Gentlemen here?

MRS SULLEN. That's his way of returning Thanks you must   180
know.

COUNT. Garzoon, the Question be a propo for all dat.

SIR CHARLES. You promis'd last Night, Sir, that you wou'd deliver your Lady to me this Morning.

SULLEN. Humph.   185

ARCHER. Humph. What do you mean by humph—Sir, you shall deliver her—In short, Sir, we have sav'd you and your Family, and if you are not civil we'll unbind the Rogues, join with 'um and set fire to your House—What do's the Man mean? not part with his Wife!   190

COUNT. Ay, Garzoon, de Man no understan Common Justice.

MRS SULLEN. Hold, Gentlemen, all things here must move by consent, Compulsion wou'd Spoil us, let my Dear and I talk the matter over, and you shall judge it between us.

SULLEN. Let me know first who are to be our Judges—Pray, 195
Sir, who are you?

SIR CHARLES. I am Sir *Charles Freeman*, come to take away your Wife.

SULLEN. And you, good Sir.

AIMWELL. *Charles, Viscount Aimwell*, come to take away your 200
Sister.

SULLEN. And you, pray, Sir?

ARCHER. *Francis Archer*, Esq; come—

SULLEN. To take away my Mother, I hope—Gentlemen, you're heartily welcome, I never met with three more obliging People 205
since I was born—And now, my Dear, if you please, you shall have the first word.

ARCHER. And the last for five Pound.

MRS SULLEN. Spouse.

SULLEN. Ribb.   210

MRS SULLEN. How long have we been marry'd?

SULLEN. By the Almanack fourteen Months—But by my Account fourteen Years.

MRS SULLEN. 'Tis thereabout by my reckoning.

COUNT. Garzoon, their Account will agree.   215

MRS SULLEN. Pray, Spouse, what did you marry for?

SULLEN. To get an Heir to my Estate.

SIR CHARLES. And have you succeeded?

SULLEN. No.

ARCHER. The Condition fails of his side—Pray, Madam, what 220
did you marry for?

MRS SULLEN. To support the Weakness of my Sex by the
Strength of his, and to enjoy the Pleasures of an agreeable
Society.

SIR CHARLES. Are your Expectations answer'd?   225

MRS SULLEN. No.

COUNT. A clear Case, a clear Case.

SIR CHARLES. What are the Bars to your mutual Contentment.

MRS SULLEN. In the first Place I can't drink Ale with him.

SULLEN. Nor can I drink Tea with her.   230

MRS SULLEN. I can't hunt with you.

SULLEN. Nor can I dance with you.

MRS SULLEN. I hate Cocking and Racing.

SULLEN. And I abhor Ombre and Piquet.

MRS SULLEN. Your Silence is intollerable.   235

SULLEN. Your Prating is worse.

MRS SULLEN. Have we not been a perpetual Offence to each
other—A gnawing Vulture at the Heart.

SULLEN. A frightful Goblin to the Sight.

MRS SULLEN. A Porcupine to the Feeling.   240

SULLEN. Perpetual Wormwood to the Taste.

MRS SULLEN. Is there on Earth a thing we cou'd agree in?

SULLEN. Yes—To part.

MRS SULLEN. With all my Heart.

SULLEN. Your Hand.   245

MRS SULLEN. Here.

SULLEN. These Hands join'd us, these shall part us—away—

MRS SULLEN. North.

SULLEN. South.

MRS SULLEN. East.   250

SULLEN. West—far as the Poles asunder.

COUNT. Begar the Ceremony be vera pretty.

SIR CHARLES. Now, Mr. *Sullen*, there wants only my Sister's
Fortune to make us easie.

SULLEN. Sir *Charles*, you love your Sister, and I love her Fortune; 255
every one to his Fancy.

ARCHER. Then you won't refund?

SULLEN. Not a Stiver.

ARCHER. Then I find, Madam, you must e'en go to your Prison
again.   260
COUNT. What is the Portion.
SIR CHARLES. Ten thousand Pound, Sir.
COUNT. Garzoon, I'll pay it, and she shall go home wid me.
ARCHER. Ha, ha, ha, French all over—Do you know, Sir, what
ten thousand Pound English is?   265
COUNT. No, begar, not justement.
ARCHER. Why, Sir, 'tis a hundred thousand Livres.
COUNT. A hundre tousand Livres—A Garzoon, me canno' do't,
your Beauties and their Fortunes are both too much for me.
ARCHER. Then I will—This Night's Adventure has prov'd   270
strangely lucky to us all—For Captain *Gibbet* in his Walk had
made bold, Mr. *Sullen*, with your Study and Escritore, and had
taken out all the Writings of your Estate, all the Articles of
Marriage with his Lady, Bills, Bonds, Leases, Receipts to an
infinite Value, I took 'em from him, and I deliver them to Sir   275
Charles.

> *Gives him a Parcel of Papers and Parchments.*

SULLEN. How, my Writings! my Head akes consumedly—Well,
Gentlemen, you shall have her Fortune, but I can't talk. If you
have a mind, Sir *Charles*, to be merry, and celebrate my Sister's
Wedding, and my Divorce, you may command my House—   280
but my Head akes consumedly—*Scrub*, bring me a Dram.
ARCHER. Madam, [*To* MRS SULLEN.] there's a Country Dance
to the Trifle that I sung to Day; your Hand, and we'll lead it up.

> *Here a Dance.*

ARCHER. 'Twou'd be hard to guess which of these Parties is the
better pleas'd, the Couple Join'd, or the Couple Parted? the one   285
rejoycing in hopes of an untasted Happiness, and the other in their
Deliverance from an experienc'd Misery.

> *Both happy in their several States we find,*
> *Those parted by consent, and those conjoin'd,*
> *Consent, if mutual, saves the Lawyer's Fee,*   290
> *Consent is Law enough to set you free.*

FINIS

AN
EPILOGUE

Design'd to be spoke in the Beaux Stratagem.

If to our Play Your Judgment can't be kind,
Let its expiring Author Pity find.
Survey his mournful Case with melting Eyes,
Nor let the Bard be dam'd before he dies.
Forbear you Fair on his last Scene to frown,   5
But his true Exit with a Plaudit Crown;
Then shall the dying Poet cease to Fear,
The dreadful Knell, while your Applause he hears.
At Leuctra *so, the Conqu'ring* Theban *dy'd,*
Claim'd his Friends' Praises, but their Tears deny'd: 10
Pleas'd in the Pangs of Death he greatly Thought
Conquest with loss of Life but cheaply bought.
The Difference this, the Greek was one wou'd fight
As brave, tho' not so gay as Serjeant Kite;
Ye Sons of Will's *what's that to those who write?*   15
To Thebes *alone the Grecian ow'd his Bays,*
You may the Bard above the Hero raise,
Since yours is greater than Athenian *Praise.*

TEXTUAL NOTES

SIGLA

1707 = [1707] edition, British Museum copy, 11775. g. 17.

1707^c = corrected 1707 reading.

1707^u = uncorrected 1707 reading.

1707^2 = undated second edition.

C = *The Comedies of Mr. George Farquhar* [1710?]. British Museum copy, 1177. f. 3.

W = *The Works of the Late Ingenious Mr. George Farquhar containing all his Letters, Poems, Essays, and Comedies published in his Lifetime* [1711]. Brotherton Collection copy, University of Leeds.

S = *The Complete Works of George Farquhar*, in 2 vols., ed. C. A. Stonehill. London (Nonesuch Press) 1930.

N = *British Dramatists from Dryden to Sheridan*, ed. George Henry Nettleton and A. E. Case. Boston (Houghton Mifflin); 1939, London (Harrap) 1949.

PROLOGUE

17 Summers] w; Summer's 1707, 1707^2, c.

25 Pictures] w; Picture's 1707, 1707^2, c.

DRAMATIS PERSONAE

18 Gentlewoman] 1707^c, 1707^2; Gentlewo-woman 1707^u.

21 *Sullen*] c, w; ~ 1707, 1707^2. 1707^2 follows each description of a character with a comma, not a full stop. 1707 supplies a full stop in each case, except after *Sullen*.

I. I

11 Coachman] 1707, 1707^2; coach-men N.

32 *March* old] 1707; *March*, Old 1707^2.

35 1706,] c, w; ~. 1707, 1707^2.

50 Years, upon] 1707; ~$_\wedge$ ~ 1707^2

60 *Bountiful*] c, w; *Bountyful* 1707, 1707^2

61 Three] 1707; three 1707^2.

64 *Bountiful*] 1707^2; *Bountyful* 1707.

66 *Bountiful*] 1707^2; *Bountyful* 1707.

67 *Bountiful*] c, w; *Bountyful* 1707, 1707^2.

161 grant 'ye] 1707; grant ye 1707^2.

162 Twenty] 1707; twenty 1707^2.

174 shew'd] 1707; shewing 1707^2.

188 Penyworths] 1707; Pennyworths 1707^2.

255 on't] 1707^2; ont 1707.

274 sadled] 1707; saddled 1707^2.

292 Gang.] c, w; ~? 1707, 1707^2.

294 Black] 1707; black 1707^2.

295   Black!] 1707; ~? 1707².
302   wou'd you] 1707; ~ ye 1707².
331   with 'em] 1707; ~ them 1707².
354   *her*] 1707²; *full stop turned in*
      1707.

II. I

16   grant 'ye] 1707; grant ye 1707².
45   Fifty] 1707; fifty 1707².
63   Tea-table]   1707;   Tea-Table
      1707².
88   Venison-Pasty] 1707²; 1707 omits
      "V".
91   naughty] s (who gives c [1707]
      as his authority); naught 1707,
      1707², c, w.

II. II

13   look 'ye] 1707; look ye 1707².
34   perswading] 1707; persuading
      1707².
40   Mark'sman] 1707; Marksman
      1707².
56   not] 1707; Not 1707².
63-4 honourable, here, my dear
      Cherry] 1707, 1707²; ~; ~∧ ~
      ~ ~ c, w; ~.—Here, ~ ~
      ~ N.
131   s'death] 1707; S'death 1707².
133   here!] 1707; here; 1707².
150   I won't tell ye] 1707; ~ wont
      tell 'ye 1707²; ~ ~ tell 'e c, w.
152   Linen] 1707; Linnen 1707².
163   the Chambermaid] 1707²; th≠
      Chambermaid 1707.
179   That's my] c, w; ~, ~ 1707,
      1707².
190   'Oons] 1707; Oons 1707².
214   Hands] 1707; Hand 1707².
220   Pound let] 1707; ~, ~ 1707².
224   *Jupiter*—] 1707; *Jupiter*,—1707².
230   you, but] 1707; ~; ~ 1707².
236   Inn-keeper's] w; Inkeeper's 1707,
      1707²; In-keeper's c.

III. I

14   Child up] 1707; ~, ~ 1707².
20   extreamly] 1707; extremely 1707²
31   Better] 1707²; better 1707.
46   was?] 1707; ~; 1707².
47   Stranger. Secondly] 1707²; ~,
      ~ 1707.
48   was, they] 1707; ~; ~ 1707².
49   was, they] 1707; ~, ~ 1707².
51   came, their] 1707; ~; ~ 1707².
52   went, and] 1707; ~; ~ 1707².
55   Why] 1707²; why 1707.
59   Because] 1707²; because 1707.
86   World; your] 1707²; ~, ~ 1707.
87   Church, my] 1707; ~; ~ 1707².

III. II

1   *Tom*, I] 1707; ~; ~ 1707².
5   *Aimwell*] 1707², w; *Aimwel* 1707,
      c.
23   starch'd] 1707; starch'd, 1707².
27   do's] 1707; does 1707².
42   I'm] 1707², c, w; I' am 1707.
47   little] 1707², c, w; litte 1707.
80-1 Regimental. You] ~, You
      1707, 1707²; ~, you c, w.
87-8 Life. You] ~∧ ~ 1707, 1707²;
      ~∧ you c, w.
101   quarter] 1707; Quarter 1707².
142   Landlord?] 1707²; ~ .1707.
147   do's] 1707; does 1707².
153   Gentlemen's] 1707; Gentlemens
      1707².

III. III

90   *Fryday*] 1707; *Friday* 1707².
123   Liquor] 1707²; Liquour 1707.
174   so contrary] 1707ᶜ, 1707²; ≠o
      ~ 1707ᵘ.
187   O le!] 1707, 1707², c, w; Oh la! N.
187   Trifle] 1707², c, w; Triffle 1707.
248   surprising]   1707;   surprizing
      1707².
248-9 well bred] 1707; well-bred
      1707².
251   Gentleman] 1707²; Gentlemen
      1707.

272 Lords] 1707; Lord's 1707².
275 your] 1707², w; you're 1707ᶜ.
286 s'death, why] 1707; ~∧ ~ 1707².
289 heark 'ye] 1707; hark 'ye 1707²; heark 'e c, w.
291 whisper] 1707; Whisper 1707².
313 Alas] c, w; Alass 1707, 1707².
324 Governour] 1707; Governor 1707².
338 Heart, and] 1707²; ~. ~ 1707.
339 him.] 1707; ~.—1707².
342 Hold, Villain] 1707²; hold, ~ 1707.
357 Sillable] 1707; syllable 1707².
358 COUNT] 1707²; Coun, 1707.
361 Oons] 1707²; oons 1707.
361 Woman] 1707²; Women 1707.
373 for't] 1707; for it 1707².
395 be vera little] c, w; de ~ ~ 1707, 1707².
410 Ruin] 1707; Ruine 1707².
411 self-Murder] 1707; Self-murder 1707².
415 unaccountable] c, w; ~, 1707, 1707².
419 pretend it] 1707²; pretended 1707.
433 Fire,] 1707²; ~∧ 1707.

IV. I

8 Ladyship] 1707²; Ladyships 1707.
15 sore] 1707²; Sore 1707.
19 Chopping-knife] 1707², c, w; Choping-knife 1707.
25 two] 1707; too 1707².
37 first, as one might say, with] 1707²; ~∧ ~ ~ ~ ~∧ ~ 1707.
42 Ha,] 1707²; ha, 1707.
69 Bountiful] 1707; Bountyful 1707².
109 Hartshorn-drops] 1707, 1707²; ~∧ ~ c, w.
129 extreamely] 1707; extremely 1707².

151 s.d. ⟨Exit GIPSEY.⟩] omitted 1707, 1707², c, w.
167 do's] 1707; does 1707².
174 Shame] 1707; shame 1707².
210 Mrs.] 1707²; ~∧ 1707.
214 don't] c, w; dont 1707, 1707².
226 won't] 1707; wont 1707².
235 a la Francois] 1707, 1707², w; à la Francois c; a la francaise N.
241 shame] 1707; Shame 1707².
253 for a] 1707²; fora 1707.
253 being] 1707ᶜ, 1707²; bein# 1707.
297 But, methinks] 1707; ~∧ ~ 1707².
303 Moisture, shining] 1707²; ~∧ ~ 1707.
338 a Plot, and a horrid Plot.—] 1707²; ~ ~, ~ ahorrid ~.—1707; ~ ~, ahorrid ~.—c; ~ ~, a horrid Plot—w.
338 First, it] 1707; ~, It 1707².
339 in't;] 1707; in it: 1707².
339 secondly, it] 1707; Secondly, It 1707².
340 in't; thirdly, it] 1707; ~: Thirdly, It 1707².
341 in't; and fourthly, it] 1707; ~: And Fourthly, It 1707².
370 s.d. Exeunt severally.] 1707, 1707², c, w; omitted N.
387 thought,] 1707; ~; 1707².
401 to ye] 1707²; to 'ye 1707.
415 O Lard] 1707ᶜ; 1707²; O lard 1707.
440 Easy] 1707; easie 1707².
448 Look 'ye] 1707; Look ye 1707²; Look 'e c, w.
506 No, Joy.] c, w; ~∧ ~ 1707, 1707².
518 do's] 1707; does 1707².
525 fey, is] 1707, 1707²; Fey; is c; Fey, is w.
525 Faash, too] 1707, 1707², c; ~∧ ~ w.
563 certainly;] 1707²; ~, 1707.
566 Affair] 1707, 1707², c, w; affairs N.

568 Enterprise] 1707; Enterprize
    1707².

577 *East India*] 1707; *East-India*
    1707².

V. I

S.D. *continues. Knocking*] 1707²; ~,
    ~ 1707.

12 Hunchback'd-barber] 1707;
    Hunchback'd Barber 1707².

23 pitty] 1707; pity 1707².

25 go to the] 1707², C, W; go the
    1707.

38 Gaol] W; Goal 1707, 1707², C.

39 lye] 1707²; ly 1707; lie C, W.

71 Life, but] 1707; ~; ~ 1707².

77 to Morrow] 1707; to morrow
    1707².

80 Fortune—] 1707; Fortune!—
    1707².

85 No, truly] 1707; ~ₐ ~ 1707².

96 *Bountiful's*] 1707; *Bountyful's*
    1707².

V. II

6   do; hey-hoe!] C, W; ~? ~. 1707,
    1707².

18 youthful, gay] 1707; ~ₐ ~
    1707².

21 *Shreeks*] 1707; *Shrieks* 1707².

29 whence] W; Whence 1707, 1707²,
    C.

43 *Shreeks*] 1707; *Shrieks* 1707².

61 leave me] 1707ᶜ, 1707²; #eave
    1707ᵘ.

67 Pshaw!] 1707; Pshaw? 1707².

71 S.D. *his Arms*] C, W; *her Arms*
    1707, 1707².

84 What do's] C; ~ does W; what
    ~ 1707, 1707².

94 spar'd,] 1707; ~; 1707².

109 Ha, ha, ha] 1707²; ~ ~ ~, ~,
    1707.

131 GIBBET.] *Gib*, 1707; *Gib.* 1707²

135 Madam, dont] 1707; ~: ~ 1707²

151 GIBBET.] *Gib*, C, W; *Gip*, 1707
    1707².

158 more, Rascal?] C, W; ~, ~;
    1707, 1707².

V. III

S.D. LADY BOUNTIFUL] 1707²,
    Lady Bountyfull 1707.

1   Mistriss] 1707; Mistress 1707²,
    C, W.

39 S.D. LADY BOUNTIFUL] 1707²
    Lady Bountifull 1707.

57 Lady, a] 1707²; ~ₐ ~ 1707.

60 Lint and] 1707; ~, ~ 1707².

61 Probe and] 1707; ~, ~ 1707².

80 Gate.] C, W; ~? 1707, 1707².

V. VI

2   will, I] 1707²; ~ₐ ~ 1707.

9   upon't, it] 1707; ~ₐ ~ 1707².

22 Proselite] 1707; Proselyte 1707².

56 propos'd] 1707²; popos'd 1707.

95 Now] 1707²; now 1707.

98 do's] 1707; does 1707².

131 *Messieurs*] C, W; *Massieurs* 1707,
    1707².

132 humble:] 1707; ~; 1707².

139 hundre] 1707; hundred 1707².

155 *Night is*] 1707; ~, ~ 1707².

156 maake] 1707; make 1707².

170 opportunely] C, W; oportunely
    1707, 1707².

174 all assist] W; assest 1707, 1707². C.

191 Ay, Garzoon, de] C, W; ~, ~ₐ
    ~ 1707, 1707².

200 *Charles, Viscount Aimwell*] ~ₐ
    ~ ~ 1707, 1707², C; *Charles*
    Viscount *Aimwell* W.

212 Almanack] C, W; Almanak 1707,
    1707².

235 intollerable] 1707; intolerable
    1707².

263 go home] 1707; gome Home
    1707².

267 thousand] 1707; Thousand 1707².

270 Night's Adventure] C, W; Nights
    ~ 1707, 1707².

271 *Gibbet* in] 1707; ~, ~ 1707².

271 Walk had] 1707; Walk, had
     1707².
274 Marriage] 1707²; Marriage 1707.
274 Bills, Bonds] 1707ᶜ; ~ₐ ~
     1707ᵘ; 1707² indecipherable here
277 How, my] 1707; ~ₐ ~ 1707².
278 Fortune, but] 1707; ~; ~
     1707².

279 celebrate]   1707²;   celebaate
     1707.

EPILOGUE

4 dam'd] 1707; damn'd 1707².
10 *Friends:*] *Friend's* 1707, 1707², c;
    Friends w.

COMMENTARY

Mr Wilks] Robert Wilks (1665–1732), actor and friend of Farquhar. Some of his greatest successes were in parts from Farquhar's comedies.

3 **Plain-dealer]** A comedy of that name, adapted from Molière's *Le Misanthrope*, by William Wycherley (1640–1716), and first produced in 1677.

6 *Active Fields]* England was at war with France in the War of the Spanish Succession, 1702–13.

8 **Union]** The Union of the Parliaments of England and Scotland. The Union was finally effected on 6 Mar. 1707; the play was first produced on 8 March.

19 *Simpling]* seeking or gathering simples or medicinal herbs.

20 *culls]* plucks.

22 *Coxcomb]* a fop or foolish person. The name derives from the jester's cap which was in the shape of a cock's comb.

I. I

1 **Chamberlain]** Servant in charge of bedrooms.

6 the *Warrington* Coach] Warrington is a town about sixty miles west of Lichfield on the road to Preston and Lancaster.

16 the *Lyon* and the *Rose]* Rooms in the inn.

29 **Tun]** A cask or barrel, holding c. 200 gallons.

32 **old Stile]** the Gregorian or New Style Calendar was formally adopted in 1582. In Britain, however, the adjustment of the calendar was not carried out until 1752, by which time the Julian or Old Style Calendar was eleven days behind that used by the rest of Western Europe.

35 **Number 1706]** Presumably a reference to ale of the previous year, 1706, in which case the ale was not fourteen years old.

42 s.d. **Glass]** Glassware.

55 **a Dram]** Of spirit.

57 **Usquebaugh]** Whisky.

61 **Tympanies]** Tumours, distension of the abdomen by air or gas in the intestine.

70 **Green Sickness]** An anaemic condition common in young girls.
    Fits of the Mother] Hysteria.

71 **The Kings-Evil]** Scrofula. It was believed that the king could cure the disease by laying his hand on the sufferer.
    Chin-Cough] Whooping cough.

87 **Whisk]** An earlier name for the card game now called whist.

90 **But he's a—He wants it here, Sir]** Bonniface implies that Squire Sullen is lacking in wit.

92 **He has it there, you mean]** Aimwell implies that the Squire wears cuckold's horns.

96 **Rent at Quarter day]** The Quarter Days were 25 Mar., 25 Jun., 29 Sep. and 25 Dec.

108 **Taxes for the taking of 'em]** The French officers are prisoners of war liberated on parole.

124 **Canting]** Double talk, from

canting meaning "thieves" (and hence allusive) language.

134 sharping] Cheating.

137 *Marrabone*] Possibly a corruption of Marylebone, then an area of London where gaming took place.

138 a good Bowler] Mr John Horden suggests to me that by this time the contrary of the proverb "an honest man and a good bowler" was itself becoming proverbial, and he draws my attention to Francis Quarles' "The vulgar Proverb's crost: he can hardly be a good Bowler and an Honest man" (*Emblemes*, 1635, 1, x).

140 in the Park] St James's Park.

150 bustle] Bestir themselves.

161 Tits] Small horses, nags.

162 Twenty Degrees] A way of indicating an area.

178 volunteering] *i.e.* for the army.

182 Counterscarp] The outer wall or slope of the ditch which supports the covered way; a term from fortification.

196 Epicures] Those who cultivate refined tastes. The word comes from the name of the Greek philosopher Epicurus (342–270 B.C.)

201 the *Indies*] Nettleton suggests "the source of their delights" as a gloss.

202 kind Keepers] *C.f.* Dryden's comedy, *The Kind Keeper: or Mr Limberham*, 1680. Keeper, one who keeps a mistress.

210 Wights] Men.

219 *Sappho*] A Greek poetess who lived *c.* 610 B.C. She was born on the island of Lesbos and "lesbian" is sometimes applied to the perverted character attributed to her followers.

221 *Acteon*] A hunter of Greek legend who, because he saw Artemis and her attendants bathing, was turned into a stag and was devoured by his dogs.

227 out of doors] Out of fashion.

237 *Venus*] Goddess of love.
      Mars] God of war.

257 fricasy'd] Cut up and served in a sauce.

262 Charge of money] An amount of money.

273 Ostler] Stableman.

283 Parliament-man] Many members of Parliament obtained their seats by bribing the electors.

358 *Cupid*] The God of love, the son of Venus.

II. I

6   *Doctors-Commons*] The College of Doctors of Law in London. Advocates practising there dealt with wills, marriage-licenses, and divorces. The charter was dissolved in 1857.

22   hospital Child] A foundling.

32   fat Ale] Strong, full-bodied ale.

34   Plaisters] A now obsolete form of "plasters".
     stilling] Distilling.

46   within the weekly Bills] *i.e.*, within London. Weekly Bills of Mortality for London were issued from 1583 to 1837.

48   *Phillis . . . Coridon*] Common names for a shepherdess and shepherd in pastoral poetry.

69   Oeconomy] Organisation, order.

108 Spleen] Ill-temper.

II. II

5   *Je ne scai quoi*] An inexpressible quality.

6 Vapours] fashionable hypo-chondria. Here a sign of gentility.

15 pimp] Procure.

23 a blazing Star] A comet.

27 Simony] "Buying and selling ecclesiastical preferments"; the term is used humorously in the sense that Aimwell is buying the "best Pue".

35 *Toftida*] Katherine Tofts. Famous prima-donna, who retired in 1709.

44 Coronation] The coronation of Queen Anne took place on 23 April 1702, five years previously.

60 s.d. GIBBET] Gallows. (also where bodies were left hanging as a deterrent and as a mark of ridicule and contempt.)

66 mourning Rings] Rings worn as a memorial of a dead person.

82 Cereuse] A white lead cosmetic.

84 paint] Use cosmetics.

87 Premisses] The articles men-tioned before.

91 Gentlemen o' the Pad] High-waymen.

96 smoak] Find out about; suspect; get an inkling of.

105 as dirty as old *Brentford* at *Christmas*] Brentford was no-toriously muddy.

124 a contrary way] *i.e.* he will he hanged.

137 whip'd out Trooper] Soldiers were flogged out of the army for some offences.

140 Catechise] A treatise for instruc-tion consisting of questions and answers. The following dialogue appeared in part in *Love's Cate-chism*. See Stonehill (1930) pp. 347–9.

190 'Oons] An oath, a contraction of "God's wounds".

224 *Jupiter*] The King of the Roman Gods.

232 *Don Quixote*] The hero of Cervantes' novel of that name (1605).

III. I

4 conversable] Ready to talk.

9 Confident] Confidant.

18 *Narcissus*] Narcissus, son of the river God Cephissus and the nymph Liriope, was a beautiful youth who fell in love with his reflection in a pool. He was changed into the flower that bears his name.

22 Cephalick Plaister] A plaster to relieve disorders of the head.

24 Steas] Corsets, stays.

39 Physick] Medicine.

42 Mercury] The messenger of the Gods.

55 Mountebank] Quack; charlatan.

70 Bag] A pouch, usually of silk, to hold the back hair of a wig.

III. II

5 *Oroondates*] A character in La Calprenede's *Cassandra*.
Cesario] From Shakespeare's *Twelfth Night*.
Amadis] Amadis de Gaul, the hero of a prose romance which was begun by a Portuguese of the 14th century and continued by a Spaniard. It was first printed in the early sixteenth century, and be-came immensely popular.

7 *Ceres*] The goddess of earth and agriculture.

14 Demi-Cannons] One of the larger kinds of artillery, a cannon with a bore of *c.* $6\frac{1}{2}$ inches.

23 brazen Engine] Warming pan.
Quoif] Coif, a close-fitting hood.

29   tickles the Trout] It is possible
to catch trout merely by tickling
them skilfully, but here the action
is akin to netting, as the fish is
already hooked.

33   Baisemains] A kiss of the
hand.

35   Orpheus] Orpheus, son of the
muse Calliope, received a lyre
from Apollo which he played with
such skill that he charmed wild
animals, rocks and trees.
        Toftida] The famous soprano,
Mrs Katharine Tofts, who retired
from the stage in 1709.

45   ingross'd] Monopolised, bought
up.

48   Frigat] A light, swift vessel.

82   in the Plantations] The implica-
tion is that he was not a soldier
overseas, but had been transported
as a felon to the plantations. The
West Indies are later described as
too hot for him. Dr Schmid
comments that Gibbet was like
the early Romans responsible for
the rape of the Sabine women.

86   Roman] In military parlance, a
Roman was a soldier of foot who
gave his pay to his captain to be
allowed to serve, and thus was,
like an ancient Roman, serving
only for the good of his country.

87   One of the first] Perhaps a
reference to the runaway slaves
who formed part of Rome's early
population.

90   Will's Coffee-House] A coffee-
house at No. 1 Bow Street, at the
corner of Russell Street, fre-
quented in the seventeenth and
eighteenth centuries by authors,
notably Congreve, Dryden,
Wycherley, Addison and Pope.

92   White's] A chocolate-house in
St James's Street, London, started
in 1697 by Francis White.

100   tack about] Proceed obliquely
by another course.

110   a Charge about me] This may
refer to a sum of money or else
to a load of powder and shot for
a pistol.

121   Drawers] of ale.

162   Teague] a nickname for an
Irishman. Louise Imogen Guiney
suggested that it was particularly
applicable to Northern Irishmen.

167   What King of Spain] In 1707 it
was doubtful whether Philip, the
grandson of Louis XIV, or the
Archduke Charles of Austria would
become King of Spain.

III. III

51   put it upon that Lay] take that
line.

53   Pressing Act] The Mutiny and
Impressment Acts, 1703, 1704,
1705, occasioned by the war. These
Acts empowered Justices of the
Peace "to raise and levy such able-
bodied men as have not any lawful calling or employment, or
visible means for their maintenance and livelihood, to serve as
soldiers". Certain offenders, for
instance debtors, were also pressed.

56   dun] importune for money due.

63   dings] flings.

68   Whore of Babylon] The Church
of Rome. (An allusion to Revela-
tion XVII. 1, 5, etc.)

129   Spleen] an upset, ill-temper, or
state of melancholia.

187   the purest Ballad about a
Trifle] This inspired Dodsley's
amusing comedy The Toy Shop
according to Charles Stonehill.

190 S.D.   Sir Simon the King] This
was a popular tune, first printed
in Playford's Musick's Recreation
(1652), said to take its name from

Simon Wardloe, master of the Devil Tavern, near Fleet Street.

212 Gold Keys] the insignia of the Lord Chamberlain, among whose duties was the control of the theatre.

213 White Rods] A white staff was carried by both the Lord Chamberlain and the Lord High Treasurer.

217 Levee] a morning reception held by royalty and the nobility on rising from bed.

his Grace] This verse is thought to be an allusion to the Duke of Ormond's failure to fulfil a promise to Farquhar.

229 Peace] Alludes to the efforts of the Tories to bring about a peace with France.

264 give no Quarter] give no respite.

265 be enter'd] entered upon action.
prevent] anticipate.

269 upon the Tapis] lit. "on the table-cloth", under discussion or consideration.

281 . . . to a dead Body] Martin A. Larson, "The Influence of Milton's Divorce Tracts on Farquhar's *Beaux' Stratagem*", *P.M.L.A.*, XXXIX, pp. 174–8, quotes from Milton's *Doctrine and Discipline of Divorce*: "Nay, instead of being one flesh, they will be rather two carcasses chained unnaturally together; or, as it may happen, a living soul bound to a dead corpse" (*Prose Works* (Bohn Edition), III, 271).

317 Parole of Honour] word of honour. The undertaking given by a prisoner of war that he will not try to escape, or that, if liberated, he will return to custody under stated conditions, or will refrain from taking up arms against his captors for a stated period (*O.E.D.*).

344 Bully] a protector of prostitutes.

358 begar] "By God."

380 Garzoon] "God's wounds."

397 fair *Dorinda*] Stonehill, *The Complete Works of George Farquhar* (1930) p. 440, comments: "I take this to be the eleventh song in Swiney's Camilla, though it does not deal with revenge, *Fair Dorinda, happy happy may'st thou ever be*, originally sung by the Baroness as Lavinia. In the third act, Dorinda herself sings a song about revenge, and the Count may have hummed bits from both. In Mountford's *Greenwich Park* there is no printed Dorinda song which answers to the description. Farquhar may have been trying to make up for his sneer at *Camilla* in the Epilogue to *The Recruiting Officer*."

416 . . . Disaffections of Wedlock] Martin A. Larson, *op. cit.*, quotes Milton's *Doctrine and Discipline of Divorce*: "God did not 'authorize a judicial court to toss about and divulge the unaccountable and secret reason of disaffection between man and wife, as a thing most improperly answerable to any such kind of trial' " (*Prose Works*, III, 263).

421 casual Violation . . . the first Lawgiver] Larson, *op. cit.*, quotes Milton: "Natural hatred, whenever it arises, is a greater evil in marriage than the accident of adultery, a greater defrauding, a greater injustice" (*Prose Works*, III, 263). Also: "They (men) would be juster in the balancing between natural hatred and casual adultery, this being but a transient injury and soon amended . . . but that other being an unspeakable and unremitting sorrow and offence. . . ."

To forbid dislike against the guilt-
less instinct of nature is not within
the province of any law to reach"
(*Prose Works*, III, 254).

425 Manacles of Law] Larson, *op.
cit.*, quotes Milton: "To couple
hatred, therefore, though wedlock
try all her golden links, and borrow
to her aid all the iron manacles and
fetters of the law, it does but seek
to twist a rope of sand" (*Prose
Works* III, 265).

IV. I

4 Where women rule] Queen Anne
was reigning at the time of the
play.

11 Mail] mile.

26 Graips] gripes, spasms.

36 Goody] a contraction of "Good
wife".

59 Receipts] recipes.

109 Hartshorn] smelling salts obtained from the horn of the Hart.

110 fair Water] pure water.

149 Hungary-water] a distilled water
from rosemary flowers.

155 *Elisian*] heavenly. Elysium in
Greek mythology was the abode
of the blessed after death.

157 *Prosperpine*] The daughter of
Jupiter and Ceres, she was carried
off by Pluto to be Queen of the
Underworld. Finally at the inter-
cession of Jupiter she was per-
mitted to spend six months of the
year in the Underworld, and six
months on earth.

159 *Euridice . . . Orpheus*] was the
wife of Orpheus who died of a
serpent bite and went to the
Underworld. Orpheus determined
to get her back, and entered Hades
and charmed Pluto with his music
until he agreed to restore Euridice
on condition that Orpheus did

not look behind him as he emerged
from Hades. When nearly free,
however, Orpheus looked back
at Euridice, and thereby lost her
for ever.

203 Originals] people who act
oddly; there is also a pun on original
works of art.

225 *Cedunt Arm togae*] the Sword
gives way to the Gown. Cicero:
Officia, I, 22.

231 *Gra*] a ghráidh, Irish for love,
dear. It became a part of stage-
Irish speech.

242 *Lewidores*] Louis d'or; a gold
coin issued in the reign of Louis
XIII and subsequently until the
time of Louis XVI.

246 *Logicè*] "according to Logic".

247 Gratification] gratuity.

274 *Leda*] Jupiter in the guise of a
Swan made love to Leda.

276 *Alexander*] King of Macedonia
in the fourth century B.C., who
proceeded by conquest as far as
India.

277 *Le Brun*] Charles Le Brun
(1619–90) a French court painter
famous for his pictures of Alexander's battles.

278–80 *Danube . . . Granicus*] Archer
compares the campaigns of
Alexander with those of Marlborough, the English general.
Marlborough defeated the French
in the Danube valley in 1704.
Alexander defeated the Persian
army at the battle of the river
Granicus in 334 B.C.

280 *Ramelies . . . Arbela*] Ramillies
is a village in Belgium famous for
the victory of Marlborough over
the French in 1706. Arbela is a
town in what is now N.E. Iraq
where Alexander decisively defeated Darius III of Persia in 331
B.C.

282 *Ovid*] Publius Ovidius Naso (43 B.C.–A.D. 18), the Roman poet, was banished from Rome by Augustus in A.D. 1 to Tomi for reasons connected with his *Ars Amatoria*, and some scandal affecting the Imperial family. He died in exile.

310 *Salmoneus*] a son of Aeolus and brother of Sisyphus, who built the town of Salmone in Elis. His arrogance was such that he caused sacrifices to be offered to himself and imitated the thunder of Zeus, who killed him with a thunderbolt and destroyed his town.

380 at the Gallows-foot] a condemned criminal's life could be saved if a woman was prepared to marry him. The Gallows-foot is the space where the relatives came to take away the body of a criminal who had been executed. But to beg a person meant to petition for their custody in the Court of Wards. The meaning is clear, that Mrs Sullen is taken, in Dorinda's view, with Archer.

421 Flambeaux] torches.

463 *Tom's*] a coffee-house famous in the 18th century, named from its landlord Thomas West.

469 Club o' th Reckoning] share of the reckoning.

470 *Morris*] the keeper of a coffee-house.

471 *Bohee*] Bohea, China tea.
     scored behind the door] probably an account kept for customers with chalk on the wall or on a slate.

476 two Acts] payment for a side-box was not demanded until after the second act, so one could then leave without having paid anything.

494 S.D. *Foigard*, a very good Name for a Clergyman] The pun implies he is a defender of the faith.

511 Bogtrotter] a nickname for an Irishman.

521–2 *Mynheer . . . sacrament*] Flemish for "Sir, I don't know what you're saying, I don't understand you, indeed".

540 *Kilkenny*] The Protestant college of St John at Kilkenny, founded in the 16th century, where Swift and Congreve were educated.

582 *enter'd him*] begun or started him drinking.

598 *Vigo*] Much valuable booty was taken in Sir George Rooke's action off Vigo on 12 Oct. 1702.

602 Tyburn] the place where criminals were executed.

604 in the Household] at Court.

V. I

57 are not Man and Wife one Flesh?] Sir Charles replies to this question in terms of Milton's philosophy. Lawson, *op. cit.*, pp. 176–7 quotes various sentences. There is no true marriage between them who agree not in true consent of mind (*Prose Works*, III, 290). The solace and satisfaction of the mind is regarded as provided for before the sensitive pleasing of the body (*op. cit.*, 188). . . . This is the rational burning that marriage is to remedy (*op. cit.*, 192).. . . . What can be fouler in congruity, a greater violence to the reverend secret of nature, than to force a mixture of minds that cannot unite? (*op. cit.*, 206). . . . Marriage is a human society . . . if the mind, therefore, cannot have that due company by marriage that it may reasonably and humanly desire that marriage can be no human society (*op. cit.*, 210). . . . The greatest breach (of marriage) unfitness of

mind (*op. cit.*, 210). . . . The unity of mind is nearer and greater than the union of bodies (*op. cit.*, 339).

72   at Cuffs] at blows.

86   All-fours] Stonehill quotes Dr Johnson's description: "a low game at cards, played by two; so named from the four particulars by which it is reckoned, and which, joined in the hand of either of the parties, is said to make *all-fours*".

V. II

31   *Alcmena*] Alcmena was the wife of Amphitryon whom Jupiter seduced by assuming Amphitryon's features while the latter was gone to war and introducing himself as her husband.

52   Ingineer] Plotter.

98   *Bedlam*] a corruption of "Bethlehem", applied to the Hospital of St Mary of Bethlehem, a lunatic asylum.

131–2   a younger Brother] a younger brother had to make his own way in the world as, under the laws of primogeniture, the elder brother inherited.

V. III

61   the Probe] a surgical instrument with a blunt end for exploring wounds.

71   *Swiss*] *i.e.* mercenary. Swiss mercenary soldiers were used as a special bodyguard by the French kings.

88   *Edistone*] The first lighthouse at Eddystone, completed in 1699, was destroyed by a storm on 27 Nov. 1703. Mr Winstanley, and several others, were lost in the building.

V. IV

4   *Hybla*] a town in Sicily, on the slope of Mount Etna, where thyme and odoriferous herbs grew in abundance, famous for its honey.

22   Proselite] Convert.

116   airy] gay, flippant.

147   *Legerdemain*] sleight of hand.

200   *Charles Viscount Aimwell*] He has previously been called Tom. See II. II. 17, 36, 41 and III. II. I.

210   Ribb] a scolding wife.

233   Cocking] cock-fighting.

234   Ombre] a card game played by three persons with 40 cards.

Piquet] a card game played by two persons with a pack of 32 cards.

258   Stiver] a small coin of the Low Countries; a coin of very small value.

267   Livres] an old French money of account divided into 20 sous.

272   Escritoire] a writing desk.

EPILOGUE

2   *Expiring author*] Farquhar was reputed to have died on the third night of the play, 13 Mar. 1707 (and on the eleventh) but he was buried on 23 May 1707. See E. Rothstein, *George Farquhar*, pp. 28–9.

9   Leuctra] At Leuctra, 371 B.C., the Thebans, under Epaminondas, defeated the Spartans: Their leader, however, was not killed there, but died at Mantinea nine years later.

14   Kite] Serjeant Kite is a character in Farquhar's *The Recruiting Officer* (1706).

15   Will's] A coffee house in Bow Street. See Commentary III.II.90.

16   *Bays*] The victor's (or the laureate's) wreath of bay leaves.

BIBLIOGRAPHY

I. Works by Farquhar

A. COLLECTED WORKS

The Comedies of Mr George Farquhar. London [1709]; [1710?]; 1711; 1714; 1721; 1728; 1736 (as *The Dramatick Works,* the 7th edition in 2 vols.).

The Works of the late Ingenious Mr George Farquhar: containing all his Poems, Letters, Essays and Comedies published in his Life-time. London [1711]; 1711 (2nd edition in 2 vols.); 1714; 1718; 1721; 1728 (6th edition); 1736 (7th edition in 2 vols.); 1742 (8th edition); 1760 (9th edition); 1772 (10th edition).

The Works, containing the *Life* by T. Wilkes, (3 vols.) Dublin 1775.

The Dramatic Works of Wycherley, Congreve, Vanbrugh and Farquhar, ed. Leigh Hunt. London 1840.

The Dramatic Works of George Farquhar, ed. A. C. Ewald, 2 vols. London 1892.

The Complete Works of George Farquhar, ed. Charles Stonehill, 2 vols. Bloomsbury (Nonesuch Press) 1930.

B. SELECTIONS

George Farquhar, (4 plays), ed. W. Archer in the Mermaid Series. London (Benn) 1906; reissued 1949, 1959.

Representative English Dramas from Dryden to Sheridan, ed. Frederick Tupper and J. W. [James Waddell]. New York (H. Milford) 1914.

A Discourse upon Comedy, The Recruiting Officer and The Beaux Stratagem, ed. Louis A. Strauss. The Belles Lettres Series. Boston (D. C. Heath & Co.) 1914.

British Dramatists from Dryden to Sheridan, ed. G. H. Nettleton . . . and A. E. Case. Boston (Houghton Mifflin) 1939; London (Harrap) 1949.

Three Restoration Comedies, ed. Norman Marshall. London (Pan Books) 1953.

Eighteenth Century Comedy, ed. S. Trussler. London (Oxford U.P. 1969).

C. *THE BEAUX STRATAGEM*

The Beaux Stratagem, London [1707]; [1707]; 1710; 1711; 1715; 1720; 1730; 1733 (8th edition); 1736; 1739; 1748; 1752; 1755; 1760; 1763; 1768; 1770; 1771; 1775; 1778 and 1798. Edinburgh 1715 (three editions); 1755 and 1768.

Belfast 1767. Dublin 1724; 1729; 1739; 1753; 1766; 1775; 1792. More recent editions include those by H. M. Fitzgibbon, Temple Dramatists 1898, Bonamy Dobrée Bristol 1929, and Vincent F. Hopper and Gerald B. Lahey, with a Note on the Staging by George L. Hersey. Barron's Educational Series. New York 1963.

D. TRANSLATIONS

*Die Stu*ʒ*erlist* (translated by J. Leonhardi). Berlin 1782.
Le Stratagème des Roués (translated by M. Constantin-Weyer). Paris 1921.
La Strattagemma dei Bellimbusti (translated by A. Lombardo). Florence 1955.
La Ruse des Galants (translated by J. Hamard). Paris 1965.

II. STUDIES OF FARQUHAR, ETC

1. The Eighteenth Century

CHETWOOD, W. R. *A General History of the Stage.* London 1749.
  "Mr George Farquhar", in *The British Theatre*, pp. 129-31. London 1750.

———. "Mr George Farquhar", in *The British Theatre*, pp. 129-31. London 1750.

CIBBER, COLLEY. *An Apology for the Life of Mr Colley Cibber, Comedian . . . Written by Himself.* London 1740.

CURLL, E. *The Life of that Eminent Comedian Robert Wilks, Esq.* London 1733.

EGERTON, WILLIAM. *Faithful Memoirs of the Life, Amours and Performances of Mrs Anne Oldfield,* London 1731.

O'BRYAN, DANIEL. *Authentic Memoirs; or, The Life of and Character of . . . Mr Robert Wilks.* London 1732.

WILKES, THOMAS. "The Life of George Farquhar", in *The Works*, Dublin 1775.

2. The Nineteenth Century

GUINEY, LOUISE IMOGEN. *A Little English Gallery.* New York 1894.

HARWOOD, THOMAS. *The History and Antiquities of the Church and City of Lichfield,* Gloucester 1806.

HAZLITT, W. "On Wycherley, Congreve, Vanbrugh and Farquhar", in *Lectures on the English Comic Writers.* London 1819.

HUNT, JAMES HENRY LEIGH. *Leigh Hunt's Dramatic Criticism.* ed. Lawrence Houston Houtchens and Carolyn Washburn Houtchens. New York (Columbia U.P.) 1949.

LAMB, CHARLES. "On the Artificial Comedy of the Last Century", in *Essays of Elia.* London 1823.

THACKERAY, W. M. *The English Humourists of the Eighteenth Century*. London 1853.

WARD, A. W. *A History of English Dramatic Literature to the Death of Queen Anne* (3 vols.). London 1899.

3. *The Twentieth Century*

ARCHER, W. *The Old Drama and the New*. London (Heinemann) 1923.

BERMAN, RONALD. "The Comedy of Reason" in *Texas Studies in Literature and Language*, VII (1965), pp. 161–8.

BERNBAUM, E. *The Drama of Sensibility*. Boston and London (Ginn and Co.), 1915.

BOAS, F. S. *An Introduction to Eighteenth Century Drama. 1700-1780*. Oxford (Clarendon Press) 1953.

CONNELY, WILLARD. *Young George Farquhar, The Restoration Drama at Twilight*. New York (Scribner's) 1949.

DOBRÉE, B. *Restoration Comedy*. Oxford (Clarendon Press) 1924.

FARMER, A. J. *George Farquhar*, in the *Writers and their Work* series. London (Longmans, Green) 1966.

FUJIMARA, T. H. *The Restoration Comedy of Wit*. Princeton (Princeton U.P.) 1952.

GOSSE, EDMUND. *Gossip in a Library*. London (Heinemann) 1892.

KAVANAGH, P. *The Irish Theatre*. Tralee (The Kerryman) 1946.

KRUTCH, J. W. *Comedy and Conscience after the Restoration*. New York (Columbia U.P.) 1924.

LARSON, M. A. "The Influence of Milton's Divorce Tracts on Farquhar's *Beaux Stratagem*", *P.M.L.A.* (1924), pp. 174-8.

LYNCH, KATHLEEN M. *The Social Mode of Restoration Comedy*. New York (Macmillan) 1926.

NETTLETON, G. H. *English Drama of the Restoration and Eighteenth Century (1642-1780)* London (Macmillan) 1914; New York (Macmillan) 1932.

NICOLL, ALLARDYCE. *A History of English Drama*, vols. I and II. Cambridge (Cambridge U.P.) 1924; 1952.

ODELL, GEORGE CLINTON DENSHORE. *Annals of the New York Stage*, 15 vols., New York (Columbia U.P.), 1927-1949.

PALMER, J. E. *The Comedy of Manners*. London (Bell) 1913.

PERRY, H. T. E. *The Comic Spirit in Restoration Drama*. New Haven (Yale U.P.) 1925.

PYLE, FITZROY, "George Farquhar (1677-1707)" in *Hermathena* XCII (1958), pp. 3-30.

ROTHSTEIN, ERIC. *George Farquhar*. New York (Twayne Publishers Inc.) 1967.

SCHMID, D. *George Farquhar, Sein Leben und seine Original Dramen.* Vienna (Braumüller) 1904.

SMITH, J. H. *The Gay Couple in Restoration Comedy.* Cambridge Mass. (Harvard U.P.) 1948.

SPINNER, K. "George Farquhar als Dramatiker", in *Schweizer Anglistische Arbeiten.* Berne (Francke Verlag) 1956.

SUTHERLAND, JAMES. "New Light on George Farquhar", in *Times Literary Supplement*, 6 March 1937.